The Concept of the Network Society
– Post-Ontological Reflections

Niels Lehmann, Lars Qvortrup and Bo Kampmann Walther (eds.)

The Concept of the Network Society

– Post-Ontological Reflections

Samfundslitteratur Press/NORDICOM

Niels Lehmann, Lars Qvortrup and Bo Kampmann Walther (eds.)
The Concept of the Network Society: Post-Ontological Reflections.
First edition 2007

© Samfundslitteratur Press/NORDICOM 2007

Cover: Frederik Storm and Thomas Thorhauge
Typeset: Samfundslitteratur Grafik
Print: Narayana Press, Gylling (www.narayana.dk)

ISBN: 978-87-593-1189-9

Published by:
Samfundslitteratur Press
Rosenørns Allé 9
DK-1970 Frederiksberg C
Denmark
+45 38 15 38 80
forlagetsl@sl.cbs.dk
www.forlagetsl.dk

Contents

Series foreword

Traditionally, politics has been understood as the ways in which people negotiate and legitimate the allocation of values in society – often focusing on the institutions of parliamentary democracy. In recent decades, however, a somewhat broader understanding has gained ground, associating politics with more diverse social goals and with equally diverse means of attaining them. Politics includes what people practice in a range of social contexts where they conceive of themselves as citizens, consumers, and cocreators of culture. The field of politics does not have one center, but is distributed, partly because of the presence of the media.

Politics is, to a significant degree, conducted in and through the media. And, the media have themselves contributed to new practices of political participation that involve a growing range of actors and interests. From the local newspaper to the internet, the media represent a meeting ground and battleground that is an integrated part of political activities involving both established and emerging social interests and groups.

This development has been addressed by a national research program in Denmark, 'Media and Democracy in the Network Society' (MODINET), during 2002-2006, with contributions by close to 50 researchers from media studies and social sciences.

The series of seven books presents the findings and implications of the research program. Each book identifies and examines a particular dimension of politics and media. From the local to the global level. Across state, business, and civil society. In the interplay between 'old' and 'new' media. And with reference to several contested notions of contemporary society as a 'network,' 'information,' or 'knowledge' society.

The book series includes empirical studies, theoretical reflections,

7

as well as policy deliberations concerning the field of media and politics. As such, it seeks to stimulate both further research and public debate on 'the network society' – what it is, and what it might become.

The MODINET research program was funded by a grant from the Danish Research Agency. During 2002-2004, it was directed by Professor Ib Bondebjerg, and during 2004-2006 by Professor Klaus Bruhn Jensen. Further information on the program and its activities is available at http://modinet.dk, which will be archived at http://netarkivet.dk.

Copenhagen, June 2005
Klaus Bruhn Jensen

Introduction

A blackbird came flying
in from the mist
it's sitting here now
singing in a wet mountain pine
soon it will fly back
into nature[1]

The mundanisation and gödelisation of epistemology

There can hardly be any doubt that the conditions for describing the world have changed. Since the turn of the 20th century at least, we have known that there is no point of observation for describing the world that lies outside the world. Even the greatest describer of the world is himself a part of the world he describes. The notion – whether it be dreamlike or nightmarish in character – that beyond the *res extensa*, the outstretched world, there should lie a *res cogitans*, a thinking entity, and that this externalised and solitary entity should be man – is no longer tenable. This was already confirmed by Husserl in his critique of the Cartesian world view, something that Heidegger and the phenomenological and post-phenomenological tradition of

---

1 Per Højholt: 'The unmistakable blackbird', *PRAKSIS, 1: Revolver*. Copenhagen 1977. Translation John Irons, © 2006.

the 20th century were cognisant of. That there should be a thought beyond the world or beyond the event in which the thought is born, is no longer a thought that can be thought. What we know about the world, we know from inside the world.

The consequences of this have been comprehensive and are still far from having been agreed on.

Firstly, it has meant that it has been possible to observe a convergence between epistemology and social science. Epistemology has been forced to concede that it cannot think of itself as a 'pure', elevated form, but is always already embedded in what – the society, for example – about, for and in which it is an epistemology. Epistemology has lost its innocence – it has become mundanised.

Secondly, it has meant that the theory of the world – to the irritation of many people it would seem – has become epistemologised. One cannot, ought at least not to be able to, devise a theory about society without considering the epistemological conditions of this theory: That one is forced to choose a position of observation within the labyrinth one is attempting to describe. And that one must adopt a stance regarding the non-ontological but autological condition that the description of society is always a self-description as well. If society is called a 'knowledge society' or a 'knowing society', the knowledge about society which the theory seeks to articulate is itself also a form of knowledge within the knowing society. If society is termed a 'network society', the societal theory itself helps constitute a network. A theory about society is always a theory about the society of society.

Thirdly and finally, it has meant that epistemology has become paradoxalised. It has, as mentioned, undergone a 'gödelisation'. For at least since Gödel we have known that a given world cannot describe itself exhaustively from the inside. The earlier, somewhat exotic Cretan Liar paradox – that it is impossible for a Cretan to argue that his statement that all Cretans are liars is true – has entered the centre of epistemology as its general condition.

This, it should be noted, is not something that certain theorists – philosophers, sociologists, etc. – have chosen in a moment of postmodernist intoxication. It is not a question of someone – for political, moral or fashionable reasons – having deselected the epistemological obstinacy of former times to adhere instead in hedonistic style to a password of epistemological arbitrariness. 'Anything goes' as the unbearable lightness of epistemology. No, it is a question of attempting – epistemologically and scientifically, theoretically and methodologically – to relate to and handle the autological conditions that theories about the world are subject to.

So it does not mean that five can now equal seven. The new conditions for epistemology do not mean that the requirements made of its powers of utterance have become weaker. On the contrary, they have become stronger. For not only must the theory – also the theory of modern society, whether it is referred to as the knowledge or the network society – account for the truth value of its statement, it must also account for the conditions of utterance for this statement.

In short: Not only has the world changed; so too have the conditions for descriptions of the world. Indeed, it can be difficult to determine whether it is the one or the other that is the case. This condition has to be taken seriously, also when it comes to the way in which the world is described, and the optic through which it is observed.

This book is a consequence of these conditions for how we describe the world. It has to do with the optic that always is involved in a description of the world. And it has to do with the consequences for the arts and social sciences that the primary ideal of first philosophy, i.e. the symmetrical correspondence between subject and object, epistemology and ontology, can no longer be uncritically accepted. What significance does this 'loss' of metaphysical guarantees – or simply certain rationales – have for the description and understanding of the society in which we live and for the epistemological tools at our disposal? The fact that the observation is always an inseparable part of the object being observed – whether it be a phenomenon, an object or a topic – can be viewed as an unfortunate conditionale that a considerable portion of 20th century thinkers have eagerly pointed out as a demonstration of the built-in frailty of the arts and social sciences.

It is, however, also possible to view the conditions as a challenge to theories and theoretical reflections. The authors of this book acknowledge the transition from an 'old' epistemology based on unity and correspondence to a 'new' epistemology that is founded more on difference and asymmetry. But in addition to this, the articles, each in its own way, seek – using sociological, philosophical and aesthetic glasses – critically to restitute, or perhaps redescribe, the epistemological potentials in such concepts as 'network', 'society', complexity' – and many more besides.

For, broadly speaking, one can proceed in one of two directions once one realises the necessity of a post-ontological perspective. One can either choose – more or less resignedly – to relativising the difference and thus never begin to track down the conditions that would still seem to be a leading principle in cognition theory. Or one can take difference thinking seriously, indeed, radicalise it, yet also retain the transcendental-analytical hold on understanding as a methodological principle. One can say that, on the one hand, it is a question of dismantling the implicit metaphysics that, among other things, determines Manuel Castells' concept of 'network' and 'network society'. But on the other hand, it is also a question of searching behind the rational and textual range of the concepts in order to study more closely – possibly basing oneself on difference – the construction that supports them. As Luhmann says, it is not just a question of what is the case but also – and more – of what lies behind.

This book is a sociological, philosophical and aesthetical study of what 'lies behind' calling present-day society a 'network society'.

The Theoretical Rationality of the Concept of the Network Society

1.

According to the Portuguese sociologist Manuel Castells, the central mark of current society is the all-encompassing use of networks, most notably digital or information technology networks. What is characteristic of these networks in the information age is that they have become more and more flexible and adaptive. They are flexible since they can relatively effortlessly alter their scale, the arrangement of their elements and the way they interact with users, machines, or other networks, and they are adaptive because they are capable of adjusting and redefining themselves through proactive contacts with their environment. Castells explains this novel change in the social order in the article "Materials for an exploratory theory of the network society", which sums up the conclusions drawn in the momentous trilogy *The Information Age*:

> For the first time, the introduction of new information/communication technologies allows networks to keep their flexibility and adaptability, thus asserting their evolutionary nature. While, at the same time, these technologies allow for co-ordination and management of complexity, in an interactive system which features feedback effects, and communication patterns from everywhere to everywhere within the network. It follows an unprece-

dented combination of flexibility and task implementation, of co-ordinated decision making, and decentralized execution, which provide a superior social morphology for all human action (Castells 1996: 15).

Two indispensable aspects of networks and network technologies can be initially subtracted from this quotation. First, Castells seems to contend that the mounting completion of flexible and adaptive technology provides networks with certain 'biological' characteristics. Networks show evidence of an "evolutionary nature"; they mature, bifurcate, and, perhaps, fade out. Second, modern networks are interactive, cybernetic systems that distribute feedback loops, thus ensuring not only communication across the networks but also "management of complexity". It looks as if modern networks are like evolving, biological systems with inborn cognitive qualities.

Not all networks are complex by definition. Nevertheless, those networks that interest Castells are pure examples of complexity. They are so in a twofold sense: What goes on inside the networks, the channelling of various content, patterns of communication, is complex; and networks, in themselves, on a structural level, are complex. Technically, this means that the relation between elements and relations as well as the relation between low and high order organization of the form of the network show emergent properties. The sum is always more than the mere totality of its parts. New media and information technologies (IT) have an inherent facility of dynamic mobilisation and an equally significant power of self-configuration. It is no wonder, then, that Castells directly relates the success of networks, socio-economically speaking, with the potentials of IT. Especially the computerization of society in a number of areas, within economy, communication, organizations, perhaps even within our mental or cognitive dispositions, allows contemporaneous citizens to cope with complexity to an unprecedented extent. However, the double notion of network complexity, as we saw above, further implies an intrinsic fragility in the concept of complexity. Is Castells primarily speaking of complexity related to the object (ontological complexity), or is he rather addressing complexity in comparison to the observation of the

14

object (epistemological complexity)? I shall come back to this question in the next section.

Furthermore, Castells insists that we are witnessing a decentralization of the very form-producing processes that create this complexity. Importance lies therefore in the *morphological* potential of networks. We have a new society. In addition, we have a new societal *form*. This form is characterized by a "space of flows". It is a form that we inhabit, and it is also a form that the managerial elite, "the networkers", can control, to some extent. Empirically, the new morphology of society based on flow can be seen in, among other things, the field of architecture (Stalder 2001). New cities are built around airports where the flow and heterogeneous co-existence of departure and arrival is more important than the identity of places. Flows create places, not the other way around.

If power comes with networks – in fact, if the dynamics of networks substitutes the hierarchical nature of power dissemination, and if networks are identified by their complexity – then power itself becomes networked, complex, horizontally scale-free and open-ended rather than vertically controlled and demarcated. As already noted by Foucault, this makes it increasingly difficult to monitor power itself, the essence or midpoint of power. No one in particular builds networks. We all do, although some take advantage of their economic and cultural effectiveness. Networks, Castells says,

> [...] constitute the new social morphology of our societies, and the diffusion of networking logic substantially modifies the operation and outcome in processes of production, experience, power, and culture (Castells 1996: 469).

The new social morphology carries with it global instrumental exchanges that selectively switch on and off individual groups, regions, and countries in a relentless flow of strategic decisions, thus operating above individual interests. Castells sees a fundamental "split" between abstract, universal instrumentalism, and historically rooted, particularistic identities (Castells 1996: 3). This division between universality and particularity is inscribed in Castells' famous hypothesis that our "societies are increasingly structured around a bipolar opposition between the Net and the self" (ibid.). One of the consequences of the bipolarity found in the morphology of the network society is alienation: "And when communication breaks down [...] social groups and individuals become alienated from each other [...] In this process, social fragmentation spreads, as identities become more specific and increasingly difficult to share" (ibid.).

So networks signify a new area. In particular the morphological structure of networks that offers a radically new flexibility and spread of both economic and cultural capital gives us a clear-sighted image of our contemporary society. Power has shifted from the Westphalian 'space of places' to a 'space of flows'. I quote Castells at length:

> Our societies are constructed around flows: flows of capital, flows of information, flows of technology, flows of organizational interactions, flows of images, sounds and symbols. Flows are not just one element of social organization: they are the expression of the processes dominating our economic, political, and symbolic life. [...] Thus, I propose the idea that there is a new spatial form characteristic of social practices that dominate and shape the network society: the space of flows. The space of flows is the material organization of time-sharing social practices that work through flows. By flows I understand purposeful, repetitive, programmable sequences of exchange and interaction between physically disjointed positions held by social actors (Castells 1996: 412).

Much in a similar vein, Anthony Giddens characterizes the modern world as being like an out-of-control 'juggernaut' that has twisted into irreversible and unpredictable global processes (Giddens 1990). Building on Paul Virilio, Sigmund Bauman depicts the nature of contemporaniety as a speeded-up 'liquid modernity' (Bauman 2000). Power is no longer concentrated within and determined by institutions such as the state, organizations like capitalist firms or symbolic controllers (media, churches, ideologies, value systems). Rather, power is 'diffused in global networks of wealth, power, information and images, which circulate and transmute in a system of variable geometry and decentralized geography' (Castells 1997: 359). While 'decentralized geography' clearly relates to the idea that nation states owe their specific ontology to nodes of a broader network of power – as when Hardt and Negri suggest that nation-state sovereignty has been transformed into a single, albeit almost unfathomable, system of mobile power, the 'Empire' (Hardt and Negri 2000, 136) – the view on 'variable geometry' is fairly more mystifying and, at best, in want of elucidation. Suffice it to say for now that 'variability' relates to the material structure of network topologies (the technical arrangement and spread of computers, wires, and protocols) *and* to the delicate concoction of technology, society and space that Castells seeks to unearth. Later on, in the third section, I shall examine the implications of geometrical and topological space in more detail.

Modern society builds on variable geometry and streams curving as intersections between organisations, networks, and people. It also represents the desire for a society liberated from friction, a society that puts liquidity, fluidity, mobility, synchronicity, and speed (or "timeless time") as primary teleological goals, and in which the greatest power and most efficient networking tools are located in the big cities. Early manifestations of this aspiration were seen in the writings of Le Corbusier, who envisioned the 'logic of the straight line' (Le Corbusier 1929 [1977]), which was later transformed into and, in a sense, completed in, Castells' notion of the space of flows.

A recent critique of this dream of spaces freed from all kinds of constraint comes from the architect Rem Koolhaas. His concept and architectural principle of "junkspace", endless buildings based on "infinite computation", is meant as a counter answer to the "debris of modernization" that disciplines the linear logic of flows:

> Junkspace is often described as a space of flows, but that is a misnomer; flows depend on disciplined movement, bodies that cohere. Junkspace [...] is an architecture of the masses, each trajectory is strictly unique [...] There is a special way of moving in Junkspace, at the same time aimless and purposeful [...] Where movement becomes synchronized, it curdles: on escala-

17

tors, near exits, parking machines [...] Flows in Junkspace leads to disaster (Koolhaas 2001).

Contemporary citizens, Castells declares, are wrought by and even a priori 'trapped' within a system of networks, networkers and network technologies. These citizens are guided and, possibly, repressed by the economically dictating space of flows. As a result, some have criticized Castells for deliberately excluding those societal groups that stand outside the streams and who constantly perceives contemporary mobility and friction-less de-territorialization as socio-cultural hindrances and monetary obstacles. However, there is a subtle difference between arguing that networks, on all levels of society, *affect* us on the one hand, and that we are always already *conditioned* by the logic and dynamics of networks, on the other hand. More and more people have access to the kind of power implanted in digital networks and similar fluid circulation and transmutation systems. A rising number of people are in a position to master or, at least, participate in the fabrication and recommencement of information. Some would assert that this is a historically novel condition where members of society enjoy a prospective for democratically 'customizing' their own lives and setting their own socio-cultural and political agenda. In accordance with this potential, Castells describes the information technology era as "a new communication system, increasingly speaking a universal, digital language both integrating globally the production and distribution of words, sounds and images of our culture, and customizing them to the tastes of identities and moods of individuals" (Castells 1996: 2).

Whether such identity making – which resembles Pierre Bourdieu's concept of "habitus" – is in reality a new mode of democracy, an effect of and, at the same time, a rebellion against the increasing globalisation, or if it is merely a powerful extension of new capitalism and the orientation towards commoditisation should not be considered further here. However, more than just a fancy catchphrase, power in the age of digital networks has progressively also become 'empowerment'. Power is being 'pulled', not just 'pushed'. This dialectic should not obscure the fact that there may still be forces in society that have an interest in camouflaging power structures in the rhetoric of empowerment.

Thus, networks are the fundamental form producing, or morphological, ontology of contemporary society. Networks are the fabric of latter-day societal structure. To sincerely follow Castells' line of argument suggests that we look closer at the concept of network since networks 'are' the society. We can understand networks as *material structures* upon which the ontology of modern day's social morphology is based. Yet, we may also choose to explain 'network' as an a priori and therefore unintelligible *condition of possibility* for each and everyone inhabiting a modern society (some of which might find it interesting to question the nature of networks).

This is a key duality rooted in the works of Castells. As with the notion of the space of flows that plainly shows both material and immaterial characteristics, the overall conception of 'networks' and 'morphology' also hinges on a double signification – it is material (or technical) and immaterial (or epistemological) at the same time.

Reading Castells does not, in my view, grant us a satisfactory clarification of how networks are structured and determined. In addition, it does not state whether the mechanics of structuralisation and determination stems from an external force, such as a society or human subjects, or whether it is the outcome of some internal design of the networks themselves. What exactly *is* a network, and how does it constitute knowledge? And, to refine the question; do networks primarily *constitute* knowledge; or are networks rather the material containers or channel systems which *enable* knowledge as is it being communicated, carried around, altered, etc.?

Following the discussion above we can pose two research questions:

RQ-1) *The concept of complexity.* Can we expose the conditionals behind the supposition of the network constituting a social morphology? First, if modern networks are actually complex adaptive, quasi-biological systems that self-organise over time in accordance with internal rules; what kind of complexity are we speaking of? Is it ontological complexity, epistemological complexity or, perhaps, organizational complexity? Secondly, if networks are most prominently carried forward by information and communication technology, does this imply that the same technology creates the social form? Can the novelty of a social morphology be reduced to the networking potentials of likewise novel technology? Consequently, we can ask, in the tradition of systems theory, if the information technologies that govern the social dynamics serving as its possible *raison d'être* must be categorized as an autopoietic, i.e. self-producing system.

RQ-2) *The concept of the space of flows.* As I briefly showed, Castells presents the idea of a space of flows that both connects to the morphology of networks and is irreducible to this morphology. Powerful networks (that additionally contain the power to empower, thus concealing their 'Empire' status) are driven by the space of flows; and yet it is not possible to decompose the building blocks of this driving force further. Evidently, the space of flows is a second order phenomenon. One observes the effects and actions of the streams, not the streams themselves. But what, one might ask, are the compulsory, underlying atoms that together make up such composite phenomena? How may we conceptualise the notion of a space of flow? More bluntly: What does the concept really mean? Is it to be thought of as the dematerialized essence of the form of the network as such (in which case it is a kind of Hegelian unity); or should it rather be considered the consequence of the mobility and de-territorializing nature of IT systems? Again, is the space of flows an *a priori* condition; or is it an observable, *aposterioric* entity?

In answering these two main interrogations two modes of enquiry may be deployed. One enquiry would scrutinize the cases and empirical substance of Castell's *oeuvre*. This has already been done in a number of sociological, economic, and politological studies. A second enquiry would critically examine the axiomatic underneath the huge amount of cases and empirical examples. Such an approach has scarcely been undertaken. Here, I will use the second model, partly because this conditionally suspicious reading might disclose something new-fangled in the reception of Castells and the rapidly expanding literature on networks; and partly since it fits quite well into the post-ontological hypotheses presented in this book, to which I shall return in the final section. I will try to unravel some of the Kantian implications of the Castellian paradigm above all by zeroing in on the explicit and implicit, technical and socio-philosophical uses and meanings of concepts such as network, complexity, space of flows, timeless time, variable geometry, and others. The following reading of the conceptual rationality in Castells must therefore be interpreted as an attempt to uncover the *transcendental analytic* level of Castells' locus, his 'paradigm'. Or, at least, I attempt to propose a set of questions capable of irritating the hitherto rather un-criticized Castellian theory. To this end, I install the Kantian framework as a methodology, *not* as metaphysics.

So, what are networks, and why are they complex? As we shall see, the question is problematic when it comes to Castells, because he often, deliberately or not, confuses a technical and a conceptual description.

2.

The general, lexical definition of 'network' is a system of lines or channels that cross or interconnect. In classical sociology, a network usually refers to a complex, interconnected group or system or an extended group of people with similar interests or concerns. Within computer science, a network is a system of computers or digital technologies interconnected by telephone wires or other means in order to share information.

While networks and networking are hardly new, what is new is that the Internet in particular and computing technologies in general are serving as the industrial driver for these electronic networks to become the pervasive and dominant organizational form of the information age (Courchene 2002). Castells describes this development in length in his book *The Internet Galaxy* (Castells 2001). Not only are networks proliferating in all domains of the economy and in society, outperforming and outcompeting vertically ordered corporations and centralized bureaucracies, but also they are finally providing evocative substance to the concept of a global economy – 'an economy with the capacity to work as a unit in real time on a planetary scale' (Castells 1996: 92).

Besides representing a new social morphology, networks are fully joined with the symbolic exchange of capital and information, both of which correspond to the global processing and distance reducing communication in time and space (Finnemann 2005: 257). In his 'Conclusion' to *The Rise of the Network Society* Castells gives the following definition of a network:

> A network is a set of interconnected nodes. A node is the point at which a curve intersects itself. What a node is, concretely speaking, depends on the kind of concrete networks of which we speak. They are Stock Exchange Markets [...] They are National Councils of ministers and European Commisioners [...] They are Coca fields and poppy fields [...] clandestine laboratories [...] secret landing strips, street gangs, and money laundering institutions, in the network of drugs traffic that penetrate economies, societies, and states throughout the world (Castells 1996: 470).

From this very basic description of networks we can extrapolate three tightly interwoven factors:

1. Understood as a theoretical term and posing as a framework for empirical analysis, 'network' becomes a *constitutive concept* that seeks to illustrate and encapsulate a new period in the course of history. Networks not only designate and compel a new mode of socio-economy; they further serve as a normative category for *the* paradigmatic sign of contemporary society.

2. Inscribed in the concept of network we also see a number of *features* that together identify the specificity of our current era. These features may be used descriptively – as is often

the case in Castells, i.e. the deliberate inclusion of both national councils and drug traffic in the quotation above – and they may further be used in a normative way, as when Castells seems to associate new democratic elements of the Internet with the overall conception of information networks and network technologies. Characteristic features of such technologies are transmutation, flexibility, adaptivity, complexity, growth sustainability, project stimulance, etc.

3. Finally, it is an inherent claim that networks must be seen as *predominant forces in society*. Societal dynamics obliges analyses that 'behave' in accordance with these forces (which clearly presupposes an epistemological model), and, as a result, the ontology of the form of the network becomes the pivotal study of enquiry. Quite often, however, this ontology is taken for granted in its most abstract and general form, thus mildly prohibiting more fine-grained studies in the organization and maintenance of differentiated networks and network models. It is quite interesting that such enquiries, in Castells' books, repeatedly pose as positive assertions (they can be falsified) while at the same time being negatively defined (they must be taken as non-decomposable, normative statements).

At this point in our examination of the Castellian paradigm it might be helpful to distinguish between two modalities: 1) the *structural organization* of networks and 2) the *socio-philosophical implications*. These implications surface from the general hypothesis of networks constituting a new social morphology. In other words, let us look closer into how Castells, involuntarily or not, combines a technological and a sociological model.

Technically formulated, a network consists of a variable set of nodes or branch points. These nodes are attached to an equally variable set of relations or 'magnetizing' forces. The union of nodes and relations then forms a pattern that can be analysed and decomposed in order to clarify the scale, structural density, or flexibility as regards reconfiguration. The analysis of the pattern is also done in order to convey the most accurate and sufficient protocol. A protocol contains the rules and encoding specifications for sending data. The protocol also determines whether the digital network uses peer-to-peer or client/server architecture. We use the term *network topology* to name the pattern composed by the variable set of links that connect to and hereby structure the organization of a network's nodes (branch points). Generally, 'topology' is a term for the geometric arrangement devices on the network. For example, devices can be arranged in a ring or in a straight line (see Figure 1). A network topology is solely determined by the configuration by which nodes are connected to each other. One distinguishes between a *physical network topology* (the cords and cables) and a *logical network topology*, i.e. the protocol. A network can be viewed as a complex entity since the affiliation of nodes and relations (and, consequently, the organizational scale of the software protocol) produces an emergent, higher order system, which makes the network more than and therefore non-reducible to the sum of its knots. This is, popular speaking, not a problem once the protocol and matching bandwidth are powerful enough.

Network complexity is thus the number of nodes and alternative paths that exist within a computer network, as well as the variety of communication media, equipment, protocols, and hardware and software platforms found in the network, i.e. network complexity is both immaterial and material. *Simple networks* usually consist of a small Local Area Network (LAN) or Ethernet with no alternative paths, a single communication protocol, and more or less identical hardware and software platforms across nodes. *Complex networks* are generally conceived as enterprise-wide networks that use multiple communication media and communication protocols to interconnect geographically distributed networks with dissimilar hardware and software platforms. *Complex pervasive networks* are even more intricate, since they not only multiply across the virtual web but also bridge the virtual space and the tangible, physical space.

Castells often implies the principal concept of complex network without discriminating it any further. However, this is not done in a stringently technical but, rather, socio-philosophical sense, as when he claims that information networks are always more than the sheer entirety of the individual interests invested in them, that they are spread across huge geographical space, and that they often deploy a diversity of protocols and other communication standards. The abstract organization of networks replaces a societal dynamics of individuals, nations, and intentions. This is what is inferred by the asymmetric relation between "the Net" and "the self" (Castells 1996: 3). One could say that the intentional ecology of old socio-economic relations is replaced by the abstract, streaming geometry of new socio-morphological networks. In the words of Bruno Latour, of whom I shall return, we should stop thinking in two-dimensional surfaces or spheres in three dimensions in favour of flexible points with in principle n dimensions relative to their potential interconnectedness, i.e. their variable degree of freedom.

We may notice then a fundamental style of *correspondence* in Castells' assertion, namely that the emergent structure of networks implying a shift from simple nodes and relations to complex, higher order phenomena shows a relationship with the sociological idea that the network morphology has a logic of its own which transcends the concrete interests articulated in each network. In short:

Higher order logic of complex network -> higher order dynamics of social morphology

As an organizational, emergent totality, the network is more than the sum of its lower level elements and relations, and the network, as an abstract fabric explaining the socio-morphological substance, cannot be reduced to the atomic level of self-interests, cooperate intentions, financial power, and the like.

Hence, a certain level of self-explanatory modality in Castells' theory is unveiled; the technical level legitimizes the socio-philosophical level, and vice versa.

What is further implied in Castells' quasi-technological description of network and network organization is the question of how the

25

variability of a node or a specific vector within the network, called A, related to B and C, is affected by the relation between B and C. The decisive significance of complex networks lies not in the distance between A and C but, rather, in the *density with which the relation between A-B-C is functionally operational*. Castells' view rests on an ideal of *network performance* that includes two balancing parts:

- *Connectedness*: the facilitation of seamless communication between the components of the network.
- *Consistency*, i.e. the variable that shows the degree of how successful the goal of the network is correlated with the inherent goal of the components.

Castells' twin categorization of network performance as well as his general explication of complex network structures unconditionally assumes the notion of *fully connected* networks, and not e.g. *star* or *bus* networks both of which would demand a more centralised power structure, one controlling the centre, and the other controlling the aggregating 'line' (see Fig. 1).

The string of argument stating an implicit correlation of technological description and sociological implications can be resumed as follows:

- A certain number of nodes, or clusters of nodes, replace singular as well as substantial interests found in old, Fordian networks.

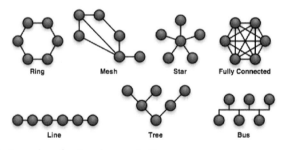

Figure 1: Examples of network organizations

- The variability structure of nodes constitutes space of flows that structurally becomes the new abstract substance of society (since the space of flows replaces the space of places).
- The social morphology of networks transcends the various interests and production of meaning articulated in the specific networks.
- Therefore, networks are more than – non-reducible to – the mere sum of the diverse traffic articulated in and through the network, and more than – non-reducible to – the sum of the relations that, precisely, constitutes the network.
- Socio-morphological networks are emergent systems since the appearance of a property or feature not previously observed becomes – or may become – a functional attribute of the system. This implies, however, that the higher-level properties should have causal effects on the lower level ones called 'downward causation'.
- But, if the network dynamics and the logic of the sociological morphology are indeed inseparable, as Castells' style of correspondence suggests, how can we then monitor any *causation* or causal dynamics – not to mention finding any '*sub*-stance', i.e. below structure or other form of vertical arrangement – that enlighten the emergent complexity of socio-networks?

So, what does ascribing emergence to the socio-morphological organization of networks mean? Networks are emergent in a number of fashions:

- Networks (as an organizational, unintelligible whole) are emergent in relation to the particular semantics that are uttered in parts of or throughout the network.
- Networks are emergent as regards the actors or individuals that further the semantic aspect.
- Networks are emergent when it comes to the local struc-

tures that constitute the construction and continuation of the network.

Thus it would appear that the socio-morphological logic of networks, *pace* Castells, transcends both a socio-psychological (or micro sociological) and a structural-functional (or macro sociological) analysis and methodology.

Using the language of complexity and emergence, Castells tries to demonstrate a delicate relation between the dynamic density of social networks and the interconnectedness of the Internet (or World Wide Web). Before fully investigating the categorical nature and level of this 'complexity', we should not fail to notice that there is a major difference between general, social networks and the networks of the Web. According to John Urry, the two can be labelled the *egalitarian network* and the *aristocratic pattern* (Urry 2004). In the former, in social networks, there is a normal distribution of individuals across the world with the overwhelming majority of people relatively weakly connected and a few moderately powerful nodes. In the latter, by contrast, a few nodes possess a gigantic number of links and they constitute totally dominant hubs across the WWW system. A nice illustration of such aristocratic networks is the global financial flows that overwhelmingly proceed through the three main hubs of London, New York and Tokyo, homes of the three most important financial tipping points and exchange markets (ibid.). Another example of an aristocratic network model is the organization of global brands as they increasingly magnify and expand their own power through multiple re-uses (Nike, Adidas, Coca Cola, David Beckham, etc.). To control a brand means precisely to (try to) control its complexity, by designing A) a system in which the evolution is very sensitive to initial conditions or to small perturbations (the current market and market strategies), and B) one in which the number of independent interacting components is large (the growth and maturity of the brand), or C) one in which there are multiple pathways by which the system can evolve (brand access and spread).

Nike is a brilliant instance of a networked company. Nike is one of the world's biggest names, internationally renowned as a major sports and fashion business. One would straight away think that this company would be very big – employing many thousands of people worldwide, yet in reality it only directly employs 22,000 people. Very few, if any, of the employees at Nike actually have anything to do with the manufacture of training shoes, instead, this operation is carried out through a range of networked suppliers throughout the world, many of whom produce products for other rival firms as well.

The key to establishing a powerful social dynamics as well as producing a financially sustainable brand strategy relies not, as one would perhaps suggest, in the multiplication of links throughout the net, but, rather, in the manufacturing of a few powerful nodes, i.e. the organization of networked suppliers as in the case of Nike. The proportion of links that is required to connect such a network together diminishes, as the network gets larger. Thus, the more widespread the network of points, the smaller the proportion of the network of those points that have to be linked through random connections. This phenomenon that travels from the social logic of relations to the com-

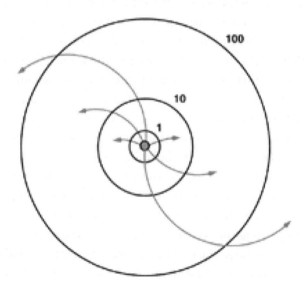

Figure 2: A node is roughly as likely to form links at distances 1 to 10 as it is at distances 10 to 100, 100 to 1000, and so on

plexity of powerful networks is known as the *small world phenomenon*. A limited number of long-range random links, if combined with densely knit lumps, produce a remarkably low degree of separation of each person from everyone else in the world. Also, this ties in with the well-known (urban) myth that everybody on the planet, whatever their social location and financial status, is separated by only six degrees of separation. Researchers have even argued that there are between 4 and 100 degrees of separation from one 'side' of the World Wide Web to the 'other'.

This seems to suggest that new information technology networks and the social dynamics overlain on top of them – or hiding underneath them – are both simple and intricate. Castells further hints at this when he explains the asymmetrical relation between *density* and *distance*:

> The topology defined by the networks determines that the distance (or intensity and frequency of interaction) between two points (or social positions) is shorter (or more frequent, or more intense) if both points are nodes in a network than if they do not belong to the same network (Castells 1996: 470).

In the chapter on "The Information Technology Revolution", in *The Rise of the Network Society*, Castells concerns himself with the cross-scientific field dating from the 1990's and onwards of 'complexity theory'. There seems, however, to be a dilemma in this kind of research. Although it by nature celebrates diversity and the intellectual cross-fertilization of science, technology, and the humanities, and thus forbids any integrating, systemic framework, complexity thinking often evolves from the desire to uncover a unified meta-theory. According to Castells, complexity theory should 'ideally be considered as a method for understanding diversity', and its epistemological value should 'come from acknowledging the self-organizing character of nature and society' (Castells 1996: 74). As an example of the uncovering of such structures of self-organization in the dynamics of society, Castells point towards the small world phenomenon, as described above. Later on, Castells underscores the idea of complexity as diversity when he concludes that 'the information technology paradigm does not evolve towards its closure as a system, but towards its openness as a multi-edged network. It is powerful and imposing in its materiality, but adaptive and open-ended in its historical development. Comprehensiveness, complexity, and networking are its decisive qualities' (Castells 1996: 75f.).

Here, we see repeatedly the couched presumption of the transparency between information technology and the logic of societal ontology. Castells dismisses the ideal of a grand, unified theory of complexity. And yet it is the underlying, abstract paradigm of 'the network' that helps organize his views regarding the modern, social morphology. In this way, the paradigmatic position of the grand, abstract 'network' in Castells' theory is implicitly accessible as a quasi-metaphysical concept and horizon of analysis. Also, he describes the complexity of socio-technological networks in both ontological (or material) and epistemological (or observational) terms. Complex networks have 'qualities'; they have a powerful 'materiality'; and yet they seem to elude our complete understanding.

Fully connected networks, i.e. wide-area, local networks or LAN-LAN bridging, and not a simple network such as the 'bus', are generically complex. One noteworthy complex feature of network machinery is the asymmetrical correlation of intersections (i.e. the variability of links tied to a few nodes) and the nodes themselves. The question is therefore if such network phenomena – socially as well as the ones constituted by the spread of communication media – are either *descriptive* or *ontological*. Are we looking at the way we look at networks? Or can we say anything about the emergent hierarchy of complex networks in themselves? Let us therefore, on a conceptual level, dig a little deeper into the field of complexity.

According to Niels Henrik Gregersen, a system is *descriptively* complex when it affords an unlimited number of descriptions that all stand in a possible truth relation to the system (Gregersen 2004: 137). We could also call this *epistemological* or *observational* complexity. It is crucial to understand that descriptive complexity has to do with the behavioural deviation by the physical system from the observer's model of it. Within the system's own ontology it may be organizationally structured, whether in repetitive or near-chaotic patterns. However, we cannot see it and therefore we lack a more satisfying, observational model that would, desirably, be transparent with the system itself. As Murray Gell-Mann writes:

> As measures of something like complexity for an entity in the real world, all such quantities are to some extent context-dependent or even subjective. They depend on the coarse graining (level of detail) of the description of the entity, on the previous knowledge and understanding of the world that is assumed, on the language employed, on the coding method used for conversion from that language into a string of bits, and on the particular ideal computer chosen as a standard (Gell-Mann 1995).

Descriptive complexity further implies that the observed parts and their possible connections to other parts within the system means more extensive models, which in turn requires more time to be computed or analysed. This feature of descriptive complexity is related to the mathematical concept of "logical depth". It is impossible, given one's observational capacity at the moment (or the computing power at hand), to deploy methods of decomposition (analysis) in the service of simplifying the complex system further without actually destroying the initial object. Logical depth refers not to the length of the most concise description of an entity, but to the length of an accurate description of a set of the entity's regularities, i.e. its behavioural pattern characteristics over time. Which is another way of saying that the ontological dynamics of complex systems cannot be modelled absolutely but rest rather on *plausible* and observation dependent criteria.

Another mode of complexity is *ontological* complexity. It refers to features of the 'real'. According to Gregersen, ontological complexity can be differentiated further using three parameters (Gregersen 2004: 139):

- A system is *constitutionally* complex to the degree that it consists of many and diverse elements.
- A system is *organizationally* complex if the constituent elements are structured into highly ordered complexes.
- And, finally, a system is *causally* complex to the degree that a given system, even if it is relatively simple in composition, is able to release many different causal trajectories by virtue of its context sensitivity (ibid.)

We can also explicate the concept of complexity by using two crucial elements; *distinction* and *connection*. The former refers to heterogeneous variety, dissimilarity, and contingency, and to the fact that there may be one or more levels or parts of the observed system that behave differently and therefore ought to be described in accordance with different, perhaps mutually exclusive, paradigmatic laws. Connection, on the other hand, corresponds to a certain redundancy, implying that different parts or levels of the complex are reciprocally interdependent, and therefore that knowledge of one part allows the determination of features of the other parts. Whereas distinction leads to chaos and entropy, connection evolves into order and negentropy (Heylighen 1996). Complexity increases when distinction and connection of parts of a system increase, since this leads to a multiplication in the variety and interdependency of the system. Overall the process of distinction and connection is a process of *differentiation*.

Thus, we can propose a general model of network:

A network system consists of *n* components, a variable set of relations, and a border, which, on the basis of differentiation and integration, unpredictability and connectedness, has the potential to increase its variety of parts and levels and its internal connections.

The process of complexification constituted by differentiation and integration can be defined as a relationship between structural and functional change:

- If a complex system (a network) has the ability to change its spatial shape and configuration we call it *structural complexity*.
- If a complex system (a network) is shaped so that it alters its temporal dimensions we call it *functional complexity*.

As I see it, there are three problems connected to the understanding and modelling of complexity:

1. First, to try to unlock the logical depth of a complex system in the attempt of expressing its dynamic regularities relies, as I have shown elsewhere (Walther 2004), on a presupposing ideal of identity, symmetry, and universality. Preferably the model should correspond to the complex system or object, and should therefore seek to repress the distinctions of the system in favour of the potential connections. We can call this the problem of *model consistency*.

2. Second, the notion of ontological complexity clearly presumes the philosophical view of realism. If it should be possible to reveal features of the real, then it is not only taken for granted that there exists an independent external world with objects, systems, and networks, but also that the task of a sound scientific enquiry is to model this external existence as accurate and consistent as possible. In other words 1) is subordinated in 2). This we will call the *realism* problem or the problem of *model-world-independency*.

3. Third, if a system or complex network is said, as in Castells, to be an omnipotent and a structurally ever-present factor to the point of totalitarianism, then we will quite logically run into the problem of *observational inclusion*. Again, the hypotheses of 1) and 2) presupposes a modelling principle as well as a philosophical standpoint which further assumes the at least theoretical or methodological existence of some external source or viewpoint that is *not* affected by the otherwise proclaimed observational inclusion. No wonder,

then, that this problem is recurrent in the history of philosophy, and especially within the realm of rational systems.

Now, if we use these concepts along with the notion of descriptive and ontological complexity in relation to our discussion of societal network complexity, two conclusions can be drawn:

1. From a *technical* point of view, communication networks possess an apparatus to produce, steer, and monitor the structural as well as functional network complexity. These tools are further defined, or limited, by the processing power, bandwidth, and protocols of the network topology.
2. Viewed in *sociological* terms, networks can only be observed and understood if they are structurally and functionally different from each other. This is obviously a problem for any 'weak' or 'strong' macro sociology because it is precisely obliged to assume the real and independent existence of objects, such as the notion of 'society', 'network', 'actors', etc., prior to any theory of spatial and temporal change.

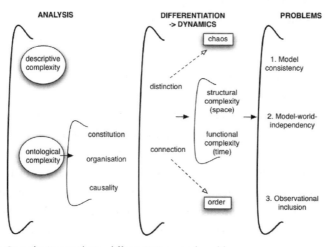

Figure 3: Complexity: analysis, differentiation, and problems

A possible reason for Castells' style of correspondence, as we mentioned earlier, lies therefore in his way of coping with these conclusions. The technical description that he often resorts to is given the role of the independent 'real', which the sociological claims – and the allegedly underlying theory – then becomes a consistent model of. But it also works the other way around. Core concepts like 'network', 'society', 'complexity', and 'space of flows' are presented as ontological categories within a vast case-oriented science system. These concepts act as functors of 'the real', thus subsuming the logical consistency of the technical descriptions.

3.

Let us go back to the concept of space of flows. In our discussion we shall furthermore pick out some key elements from Bruno Latour and relate them to the Castellian paradigm. In a certain sense, Latour can be said to radicalize ideas that are already inherent in Castells. Thus, equipped with a proper dosage of Latourianism, we might be able to 'save' the theoretical rationality of Castells' network concept.

From the point of view of social theory, Castells says, "space is the material support of time-sharing social practices" (Castells 1996: 441). Following this characterization, Castells defines the space of flows as the material organization of time-sharing social practices that work through flows. The concept of flow must be understood as iterative and controllable sequences of exchange and interaction between physically "disjointed positions held by social actors in the economic, political, and symbolic structures of society" (Castells 1996: 442). In an almost neo-Marxist fashion, Castells insists that the space of flows is largely characterized, or 'filled', by the prevailing social practices. It is these practices that play a "strategic role in shaping [...] society at large" (ibid.).

It is the space of flows that determines the social structure and social morphology. The social interests that are expressed in and through the flows become less powerful (Finnemann 2005: 267). The real power, therefore, is revealed in the "timeless time" and in "the precedence of the flow of power over the power of flows". This timeless time

> [...] belongs to the space of flows, while time discipline, biological time, and socially determined sequencing characterize places around the world, materially structuring and destructuring our segmented societies. Space shapes time in our society, thus reversing a historical trend; flows induce timeless time, places are timebounded [...] The space of flows [...] dissolves time by disordering the sequence of events and making them simultaneous (Castells 1996: 466f.).

According to Castells, three "layers" can describe the space of flows. A circuit of electronic exchanges constitutes the first layer. The nodes and hubs of the space of flows identify the second spatial configuration or layer. While places in the first layer are non-existent, as their positions are solely defined by the exchanges of flows in the network, nodal configurations link up specific places that display social as well as functional characteristics (Castells 1996: 443). And while hubs usually serve as a coordination of communication across the network, nodes essentially serve as strategic centres and locality-based organization. The third layer of the space of flows is the spatial structure of the dominant, managerial elites. The elites are the controlling agents that exercise the directional function "around which such space is articulated" (Castells 1996: 445).

When the space of flows appear uncontrollable, societies tend to recover their identity – otherwise swallowed by the flows – by constructing material and immaterial symbols that expose their own reality. This is predominant in postmodern architecture, the erection of buildings that wish to restore the sense of geographical place, historical specificity, and cultural solidity (Castells 1996: 449). However, as Castells notes, the meaning of these messages conveyed in architecture "will be lost in the culture of 'surfing'" (ibid.). The architecture that seems most suited for a contemporary space of flows becomes "the architecture of nudity", one "whose forms are so neutral [...] that they do not pretend to say anything […] they confront the experience with the solitude of the space of flows. Its message is the silence" (Castells 1996: 450).

The space of flows is defined by Castells as a new "variable geometry" as well as a "topology" that designates the morphology of the network society. As for the first term, variable geometry, it is actually a technical term used in e.g. aircraft engineering which explains the alterations of planforms of planes (also referred to as the "swing-wing principle"). Clearly, this is not Castells' point here. Rather, he is in line with various vague sociological claims that our current society is increasingly abandoning metric distances, places, nations, and borders in favour of globalized interaction between disparate groups of people, decision makers, and the like. The variability implied here refers to the growing de-territorialization of our world and to the increasing speed with which communication travels from one place to another, with the total disruption of the actual 'here' and 'now' as the primary teleology.

As for the second term, topology, it is scientifically fruitful to think of complex, societal networks as topological systems. Topology investigates the attributes of the spatial, which secure continuity for objects as they are displaced through a space (Law 2003), and it can be seen as a radical transformation of Euclideanism. Objects with three dimensions are imagined to exist precisely within a conformable three-dimensional space. They may be transported within that space without violence so long as they do not seek to occupy the same position as some other object. And so long as their co-ordinates are sustained, they also preserve their spatial integrity, and so they can be definitely pinpointed in a model using Cartesian coordinates.

A network, however, is in itself a general topological model. For in a network, elements retain their spatial integrity by virtue of their position in a set of links or relations (Law, ibid.). Object integrity, then, is not about a volume within a larger, absolute Euclidean volume in which the space coordinates spread evenly in all – geo-metric – directions. It is rather about holding patterns of links stable. The transgression of Euclidian geometry lies in the existence of spaces or spatial models where fixed, metric distances cannot define proximities since distances do not remain fixed (Delanda 2002: 23).

Actor Network Theory (ANT) studies objects, most notably objects that are the effects of an array of relations, i.e. of a network. Thus, ANT concentrates on networks, and more precisely the interaction between humans and non-humans that construct society. Predominantly Law, Callon, Latour and Serres pioneered this relatively new theory amongst others. They argue that geographical scale (global, national, regional, local) are interwoven together through the complex nature of reflexive connections between and through humans and non-humans.

While Castells in *The Rise of the Network Society* focuses on the nodes of the network that administer information flows, i.e. international cities, organizations, and financial centres, ANT, and especially the seminal books by Latour, directs our attention to the flows or, as Latour names them, the "immutable mobiles" themselves (Latour 1990). These "mobiles" are the integral components that stabilize the relations of a network. Paradoxically, however, the mobiles are also conditioned by sets of relations. The mobiles are, one could say, capable of mobility, yet also conditioned by mobility. It is this fact that makes them impossible to 'ground' within a traditional, ontological framework. (And in this respect they resemble the concept of "the fold" in Deleuze). Writing in a post-structuralist wave and in the tradition of Guattari, Deleuze, and the late Foucault, Latour proposes a theory that describes the underlying mechanisms attached to any kind of transformation and process of interaction in society. However, it is a theory that, at the same time, acknowledges the unintelligibility – meaning the constant dissemination and rapid movement – of the relations, which define the identity of networks.

If Castells' view on network can be understood mainly as a *nodal network*, a theory that above all seeks to illuminate the new power-nodes and power-hubs in the flows of society, then Latour's ANT can be described as a *relational network*. The two modes of network, nodal and relational, correspond to, respectively, *ontological complexity* and *observational complexity*. In ANT, a network is composed of actors who define the network. However, the rationality or ontological identity of these actors can only be explained by the contingent position of the actors themselves, who are, in the first place, determined by a set of contingent relations. Thus, the network comprises the actors and their variable relations, but the actors are far from being stable entities – rather, they are disseminating, relational objects.

The pivotal difference between Latour and traditional macro-sociology, including Castells, is not that humans and non-humans are treated symmetrically as stable entities in a given social semiotics and eco-social dynamics, but that they are defined relationally as integral functors in the network. It is therefore not the ontology of the network that defines and determines the structural position and functional quality of human and non-human actors, but instead the relational 'dimensionality' of the actors and the possible epistemologies they possess that constitute the network. In conclusion, this leads to a relational epistemology in Latour that rejects the naive positivist view of objects or actors as existing in themselves prior to any participation in eco-social and semiotic networks of interactions.

Although Castells seem to acknowledge observational complexity as a modality of modern networks, he nevertheless stresses the importance of discriminating nodes and hubs which, being both inside and outside the networks, operate as external power factors in the management of communication and space of flows. Latour, on the other hand, is very much in line with the systems theory of Humberto Maturana and Fransisco Varela and the concept of "autopoiesis" or self-formation later developed in the social theory of Niklas Luhmann (Luhmann 1995). According to Maturana and Varela (1980), an autopoietic system fulfils six criteria:

- The system needs a border to make it identifiable.
- It needs components so that the system is analyzable.
- The interaction of the components can be described in general physical laws, in other words, the system is a natural system.
- The boundary is self-maintained by preferential neighbour-

hood relations. The system, therefore, can stabilize its own boundary.

- The systems is contained within and producing the boundary.
- The system is self-productive. The system uses only its own components or transformed imported components.

Just as the network is constituted by the actors and relations that are the product of the relations that formed the actors in the first place, the network shapes and maintains itself out of its own components – and in this sense it is autopoietic. Systems theory is especially well equipped theoretically to explain the process of boundary management and internalization in networks. The crucial elements in this respect are environment and structural coupling. While environment is that 'something' that influences the network yet not actively controlling the inside of the network, structural coupling refers to the dynamic process with which elements of the environment are translated into the network. These elements are then determined by the codes and functional characteristics of the system (or network) itself. Thus, the dynamic evolution of network, and the possible communication between them, occurs as the result of entirely functional, systemic principles, and not physical.

4.

If I understand Latour correctly, Actor Network Theory can be conceived as a way of paving the way for a post-ontological understanding of 'network' and 'network society'. The crucial claim of post-ontology is that we ought to stop thinking of objects as solely ontic, that is, self-identical, stable entities. In a way, post-ontology takes Heidegger's *Seinsvergessenheit* – the claim that philosophy has "forgotten" the difference between the ontic, being, and the ontological, the being of being – seriously. Rodolphe Gasché interprets the ontic-ontological difference thus:

> The difference between Being and beings is the difference between Being as
> the horizon whose opening makes it possible for beings to appear within it,
> and beings as those things which appear and come to stand within that hori-
> zon itself (Gasché 1994: 91).

However, it is a rather radical continuation of Heideggerianism, since post-ontology exactly believes that we *should* forget the metaphysical stance of *any* ontological ground. What we moreover *ought* to do is critically investigate the complications of the simultaneously repressed and "opening" metaphysics of quasi-ontological claims – such as the ones made by Castells – *and* make enquiries into how systems *do* work despite the fact that they *cannot* work if they are thought of as traditional identities. Consequently, we should forget ontology as metaphysics; but we should not forget the kind of studies that try to uncover the methodological and functional consequences of theories – like Castells' – that *act* as ontologies or, at least, receive a certain 'aura' of bullet-proof truth statement.

Post-ontolological thinking invites us instead to be more attentive towards the difference and relational functionality that constitute objects. This functionality, however, can never be grounded in ontological rationality, cleverly disguised as a new kind of socio-philosophical and quasi-technical metaphysics, but must instead be explained by the observational characteristics of systems that manage their own border and formation of components. Networks function by means of their internal relations; and the only way to grasp this functionality is to analyse the differentiation of the relations themselves as well as the differentiation of the 'inside' and 'outside' of the network system – both of which are internalised within the system if the system is to be 1) functionally operative and 2) capable of performing structural coupling with other network systems.

This further implies that network objects can never be steady configurations since they are always already conditioned by 1) the contingency of an observer, as we saw in our discussion of epistemological complexity, and 2) the inherent, necessary difference of the system itself. It is a vital claim of post-ontology that a system (a network, an object, or an entity) can only be conceived *as* a system if it is different from itself. The system S is and is not, simultaneously, S and not-S. Otherwise the system could not account for what is being internalised within its own boundaries; in short, the system would not be able to manage the border and the complexity it contains. Knowing a system means to act from within the horizon of the system itself (Walther 2004). But for this epistemic activity to be effective, a system must be functionally different from itself. S thus paradoxically equals S', not S, S-mark. When disease is overcome, the biological system (the organism) enters a different state, it differs from itself, and yet it is the very same system. In other words: the system is nothing else but the distinction of the system from its environment. In fact, a system is not even the 'world' *inside* the system (idealism) nor is a system a more or less consistent model of the outside world (materialism). Instead a system is the *distinction* that functions as the indication or 'marker' of future structural coupling by which the system is functionally operative. By definition, and if this is correct, then systems *are* networks, and networks *are* furthermore autopoietic collections of dynamic elements and relations. We can monitor how these systems operate; we cannot, however, uncover their true ontological status.

We began this article with the hope of seeking out the a priori conditionals of the dynamics of networks. As we have seen, such conditionals disseminate into the paradoxical logic of systems that operate on the basis of difference. At the same time, however, it seems impossible to reveal this difference in any absolute categories. Several explanations in Castells' writings of our modern network society seem designed to unveil the complex or simply confusing play of almost unfathomable economic and cultural transformation. In empirical terms, it does so quite impressively. What is revealed, then, is not the inner essence of networks, nor the systemic functionality of their operational capacity, but, rather, a certain blend of technological description, a hyped and hyperbolic definition of the power of flows as the contemporary complexity handling tool, and, finally, an ontological and even metaphysical positioning of the unified theory of 'network' as the fitting horizon for the many ontic analyses and cases.

References

Bauman, Z. (2000). *Liquid Modernity*. Cambridge: Polity Press.

Castells, M. (1996). *The Rise of the Network Society*. Oxford: Blackwell Publishers.

Castells, M. (1997). *The Power of Identity*. Oxford: Blackwell Publishers.

Castells, M. (1998). *End of Millenium*. Oxford: Blackwell Publishers.

Castells, M. (2001). *The Internet Galaxy*. Oxford: Oxford University Press.

Courchene, T.J. (2002). Manuel Castells and the New Economic Order. In *Proceedings of Network Worlds Symposium*, Quenn's University.

Delanda, M. (2002). *Intensive Science and Virtual Philosophy*. London: Continuum.

Finnemann, N.O. (2005). *Internettet i mediehistorisk perspektiv* [The Internet in Media Historic Perspective]. Copenhagen: Forlaget Samfundslitteratur.

Gasché, R. (1994). The Eclipse of Difference. In *Invention of Difference*. Cambridge, Mass: Harvard University Press.

Gell-Mann, M. (1995). What is Complexity? In *Complexity*, vol. 1, no.1.

Giddens, A. (1990). *The Consequences of Modernity*. Stanford: Stanford University Press.

Gregersen, N.H. (2004). Complexity: What is at Stake for Religious Reflection? In K. v. Kooten Niekerk and H. Buhl, *The Significance of Complexity*, Burlington: Ashgate.

Hardt, M. and Negri, T. (2000). *Empire*. Cambridge, Mass: Harvard University Press.

Heylighen, F. (1996). What is Complexity? In *[internet]*.

Koolhas, R. (2001). Junkspace. The Debris of Modernization. In C.J. Chung, et al. (eds.), *Harvard Design School Guide to Shopping*. Köln: Taschen Bücher.

Latour, B. (1990). Drawing Things Together. In M. Lynch and S. Woolgar (eds.), *Representation in Scientific Practice*. Cambridge, Mass: MIT Press.

Law, J. (2003). Topology and the Naming of Complexity. In *[internet]*.

Le Corbusier (1929 [1977]). *The City of Tomorrow and its Planning*. London: The Architectural Press Ltd.

Luhmann, N. (1995). *Social Systems*. Stanford: Stanford University Press.

Maturana, H.R. and Varela, F.J. (1980). *Autopoiesis and Cognition*. Dordrecht: D. Reidel.

Stalder, F. (2001). The Space of Flows: Notes on Emergence, Characteristics and Possible Impacts on Physical Space. In *5h International PlaNet Congress*. Paris. In *[internet]*.

Urry, J. (2004). Small Worlds and the new 'Social Physics'. In [*internet*].

Walther, B.K. (2004). Big Theory – Strong Theory: The Ontological Ghost of Post-Ontological Epistemology. In *Cybernetics and Human Knowing*, vol. 11, no. 3.

LARS QVORTRUP[1]

Network, Knowledge and Complexity

Introduction

This article has two main aims.

One is to present a critique of the theory of the so-called network society, in particular with the treatment of it in Manuel Castells' three-volume work. This is not a critique of detail, one that accepts the basic framework but contends some specific observation or other. Nor is it the critique of an outsider who – in, for example, an ideological way – criticises the network paradigm for being what could be called a 'false' paradigm. It is rather an analysis of the network society as a name that society has given itself in order to be able to talk about itself as a society. The 'network society', in other words, is seen as a communicative trick, an address that society has given itself. And the trick has worked well, it has to be added, when one considers just how popular this address has become.

It must have been obvious ever since Gödel that no society can reach itself via its own operations (cf. Luhmann 1997: 866). Society *an sich* is not accessible from the outside. This does not, however, deny

---

1   This article is based on a lecture given at the MODINET workshop on 26-27 March 2003 on the network society and the concept of the network. My thanks to Bo Kampmann Walther for his comments on an earlier version of the paper.

that society has a need to turn the concept of society into a communicative trick for the societal discourse. There is, then, a need to designate society as such. This Luhmann refers to as the self-descriptions of the social system, known to us from early European categorisations of society as society up to the latest categorisations of society as 'postmodern' society. The 'network society' is such a self-description.

The second aim is to take the actual category 'network' seriously.[2] In any social system there is a network, if by network one means nothing else – or more – than social relations between individuals. In that sense, networks are to be found in interactive systems, organisational systems and in societies. Unless one claims that 'networks' characterise a particular type of personal relations and asserts, for example, that hierarchical relations are not network relations, it is therefore not a qualification in itself to call a society a network society. But if one attaches a particular sociological status to networks – which Castells does[3] – one naturally has to ask oneself the question what it is that distinguishes networks from other forms of social relations, just as one could possibly have the ambition to trace a categorisation of types of network. I intend to do this, since my assertion is that there is a link between the concept of knowledge and that of network. My ambition, in other words, is to identify a system of forms of networks.

2   See for example Dirk Baecker, who defines networks as a re-entry relation between control and identity. Networks are characterised by being a control-based relation that is based on attributions of identity. The relation between you and me is controlled by our mutually attributing identity to each other (Baecker 2005: 226).

3   That is what Manuel Castells attempts to do when he defines networks as '...open structures, able to expand without limits, integrating new nodes as long as they (...) share the same communication codes (for example, values or performance goals).' (Castells 1996: 470). With this definition, Castells is not all that far removed from Luhmann's concept of differentiated functional systems. A further link can perhaps also be made between Castell's relation between networks and 'space of flow' (which is defined as 'society': 'Space is not a photocopy of society, it is society', ibid: 410) and Luhmann's relation between function systems and society. For 'space of flow' see also Dirk Baecker 2005: 208.

The 'network society'

What is it that causes some people to call present-day society a 'network society'? Is it possible to capture any distinctive characteristics of this particular epochisation of society? And if it proves possible to identity anything significant in terms of epoch about the period in which we live, is the concept of 'network society' particularly suitable for solving this task?

In order to answer these questions it is not sufficient merely to observe 'something', i.e. a society or sections of a society. It is also necessary to observe observations of society. The question is not what this society 'is' but how it can be designated. Why has Castells enjoyed such great success with this concept, and why has it spread to Davos, government commissions, journalism and political language – even to research programmes? This is one side of the question. The other is whether one could also – or instead – use other terms, and what effect on people's understanding that would have.

Formerly, such a project would have been defined as ideological criticism. The 'network society' would have been seen as an expression of a false consciousness, behind which there lies a second truth that only researchers are able to reveal – that is what people would earlier have believed.

I do not agree with this programme. Concepts too, no matter how much like 'newspeak' they appear to be, are a part of the reality of society. Even so-called 'false' consciousness is consciousness in society about society. To use a term – one that from another observational position appears to be 'false' or 'superficial' – is to create a distinction, i.e. to distinguish something from something else and thereby reduce contingency to something that can be named. That, as some people claim, there exists a 'superfluity' of discourses is then an expression of the fact that in modern society there is a need to produce many distinctions. In such a situation it is an illusion to believe that behind the facade there should be anything else hidden than a second facade, behind the one discourse anything else that a second discourse. So the investigation ought not be focusing on trying to reveal false discourses via what must therefore implicitly be assumed to be a true discourse. It ought to be focusing on the description of this system of discourses (one of which is the scientific discourse through which other discourses are described), with the aim of asking whether this actual situation of reciprocal descriptions and re-descriptions contains a significant expression of society.

In other words, it is an illusion to believe that behind the surface there is a truth. This is a Marxist or Freudian paradigm – behind the false consciousness one finds the true working-class consciousness, behind the ego there is the super-ego, and both parts are accessible to the piercing scientific gaze – which today is of interest only in the sense that it represents a further discourse in society that one can observe. Indeed, it can hardly be denied that even the spatial metaphorics for 'surface' and 'depth' is a discourse, even though a research discourse, and that even the contribution made by researchers to what is true and false about society – including if and how it is a network society – is a discourse in society that ought to be observed. When someone claims that society is characterised by its surplus of discourses, it is a self-contradiction to believe that precisely this assertion is stated from a free and neutral space in terms of statements. That scientific utterances – those of experts – play an important role in a multi-discursive society such as modern society ought therefore to be included as a part of the investigation of modern society. Suddenly, the TV team is standing outside the research lab – and out teem the experts in order to add their voice to the multi-discursive chorus.

What is the case – and what lies behind it?[4]

As has already been emphasised, my point of departure is that even

4   The following section is inspired by Niklas Luhmann's article "'What is the Case' and 'What Lies Behind It'? The Two Sociologies the Theory of Society" (Luhmann 2000 [1993])

when scientists describe society, they do so from a position within society. It is hard to quarrel with that.

From this it can be deduced that nor can sociology, as Luhmann writes, 'understand itself as an independent instance of reflection that helpfully or critically can instruct society as if it came from outside.' (Luhmann 2000: 17) Sociology and other sciences that describe phenomena in society also therefore contribute to the chorus of social self-descriptions. Politicians describe society. Journalists describe society. Lawyers and businessmen, workers and employers, teachers and students, immigrants and clergymen describe society – although they do so in different ways. And even media researchers, sociologists, politologists, etc. do so. There is no specially privileged position outside the chorus, and there is no one who has special access to indicating the concert pitch, in relation to which the others are singing out of tune.

But what, then, is to be done? Sing along as loudly as one can, or remain silent and let the others bawl away? No, but one could start by finding out how the scientific description of society comes about. For here science differs from other descriptions of society: It is conscious of – indeed, is interested to a particular extent in – the criteria for its descriptions of society, knowing very well that these criteria are not incontestable either. It spends time and resources on observing its observations.

So one is not to stop making one's observations, but one must supplement them with self-observations, just as in the observation of the descriptions of society made by journalists, politicians, officials and citizens one is interested in the question of just how precisely these and not other descriptions come into being.

In relation to this, the question usually arises whether this cannot become a self-description circus *ad infinitum*. Does one never reach the 'final' or 'definitive' description? The answer is of course that one does not – and that the actual question represents an illusory expectation. What one does, though, is to describe a social polyphony, which is both interesting as a characteristic and also ought to be evaluated in terms of function. The question of when 'the truth' is reached can, for example, be replaced by that of descriptive stabilisation. And in that case, the stabilisation does not lie in there being a 'foundation', but in the fact that the many discourses, the polyphonic voices, reciprocally stabilise each other, i.e. establish a state of temporary stability that is determined by the complexity of the situation. Between chaos and order one finds the state of dynamic stability which, to use Per Bak's expression, can be called self-organised criticality (cf. Bak 1996).

The distinction between phenomenon and cause

To be able to make an observation one first has to make a distinction. One has to know what the criterion of observation is. Only via this is it possible to focus on something and leave other things aside.

But what, then, is the basic observational distinction of social science, or – to use a looser term – its 'discourse', i.e. the way in which it talks about the world? My assumption is that the discourse, as already mentioned and proposed by Luhmann (Luhmann 2000 [1993]), is formatted on the two questions 'What is the case?' and 'What lies behind it?' In other words, that the distinction via which the world is made observable is that between phenomenon and cause. One must therefore assume that the actual separation of one's observation of society and the posing of these two questions underlie the scientific discourse, which therefore ought to be observed critically. The standard mode of procedure in social science is to list data and to look for explanations – indeed, causes – of these data. Something 'appears' to one in a particular way. Something is the cause of this appearance. On the face of it, one would therefore claim that the social scientist first observes (makes a distinction between 'being' and 'non-being') and then reasons. It seems more reasonable to me, however, to claim that the social-scientific observation is the particular observation that is based on the distinction between 'What is the case' and 'What lies behind it' and that qualifies this distinction in the insistence on truth: For 'What lies behind it', i.e. the indication of 'the cause', contains 'the truth' about 'what is the case'. It is this particular way of looking that distinguishes social science from politics.

This distinction can be made in many different ways and comes into expression via many metaphors. A well-known metaphor is the spatial: One distinguishes between surface and depth. A second is the temporal: One distinguishes between present and past. A third is the causal: behind the effect lies the cause. However, the relation implied here can vary. Some people claim that there is a direct link between surface and depth, effect and cause, i.e. that the effect is a function of the cause. Such people are sometimes called positivists. Others claim that there is a converse or negative link: That what we think we see is distorted by the underlying cause. These people are sometimes called critical thinkers. They look out for false consciousness and, because their basic observational distinction is an inversion of the positivist observational distinction, they form a perfect alternative to positivism. No one, it can be claimed, can quarrel with each other so perfectly as representatives of positivism and critical thinking, since they are mirror images of each other.

The social-scientific observational distinction can, however, be fleshed out in different ways, depending for example on what one places in the foreground. What is the inside of the observation and what is its outside? What is sharply in focus and what is in the background? So I want now to name two examples of how this observational distinction is formatted: The empirical distinction, which places 'What is the case?' in the foreground; and the metaphysical distinction, which places 'What lies behind it?' in the foreground.

The empirical distinction

How does science tackle its observational problem, that society is observed from a position within society? It does so – among other things – by asking and thereby distinguishing between precisely these two questions. It probably does so most obviously in the form of so-called empirical research.

One finds a so-called representative phenomenon, i.e. a phenomenon that at the same time is claimed to be significant and valid – and that of course also must be accessible to the researcher who is to carry out the investigation. Taking examples from Castells' analysis of the network society, this could be the development of the employment structure in the G7 countries in 1920-2005 (Castells 1996: 207f), the French Minitel project (ibid: 343f), Zapatistas in Mexico (Castells 1997: 72ff), American feminism (ibid: 176ff), the formation of a national state in Singapore (Castells 1998: 246ff), etc. In other words, one assumes to answer the question: 'What is the case?', implicitly knowing – but simultaneously hiding – that other ways of selecting and observing would naturally have produced different results. Answering 'what is the case' thus contains an invocation that can neutralise demons.

When that has been done, one begins with question two: 'What lies behind?' Here the critical questions may be asked. Here one can reveal that the data are unequally distributed – they always are – e.g. that there are more women than men, semi-skilled than skilled, old than young, immigrants that indigenous, etc. that have incomes beneath the average, are on social security, feel sorry for themselves, do not have access to the Internet – or whatever one should choose to ask about. The result, in other words, is in one sense determined in advance: Imbalances and unequal distributions can be revealed, which means one has already almost answered the second question: What lies behind? Differences lie behind.

As already said: In reality this method of first choosing 'facts' and then 'explanations' helps one to avoid the intriguing problem that these scientific observations could also have been made differently. Luhmann says it in the following way: it is precisely the separation of the two questions (what is the case and what lies behind?) that saves science from reflecting its own unity, i.e. saves it from having to relate to the fact that every observation, even the most 'empirical', is based on a certain focusing and angle (Luhmann 2000: 11). First, 'society' speaks, and the researcher remains silent (as if society does not precisely 'speak' because it is being observed on the basis of specific assumptions). Then society remains silent while the researcher speaks (as if the speaking done by the researcher is also not part of society's self-comment).

So what can one do? It does not help to cut the Gordian knot (not in this case, at any rate). But one can at least describe how the knot has been tied. We must, know how our observations are made, and we must use resources for precisely that question. For from another perspective it may not be nearly as interesting whether 12% or 17% of Danish citizens are on the Internet every day as it is that someone finds precisely this question interesting.

It is often easier to see this point if one looks at something that lies further away. The interesting things about the non-discussed and quite generally accepted observations and explanations to do with race in the beginning of the 20th century is presumably the way in which the questions were devised and the general acceptance they gained. The most interesting thing about the scientific observations of 'savages' at the end of the 18th century is hardly whether they wore two or three feathers but the pre-assumptions with which those early European anthropologists set out to study these strange phenomena.

The metaphysical distinction

It is possible to separate the two questions by carrying out so-called empirical research. But they can also be separated metaphysically. It is possible to identify the metaphysical entity that fleshes out the question 'what lies behind it' and give it a name.

One exceptionally clear example of this move is to be found in the legal philosopher Carl Schmitt (which is a crucial reason for why he is so interesting: He makes clear the metaphysical move of social science).

Throughout his long academic career, Carl Schmitt[5] was interested, among other things, in sovereignty and how it is represented. Sovereignty was 'the secret' behind democracy, he claimed, for what is it that determines a state of emergency – which is the state into which democracy steps in order to protect itself? It is: The sovereign.

'The sovereign is the one who decides over the state of emergency'

---

5   The following is based on the special issue of the periodical *Distinktion* on Carl Schmitt, cf. Distinktion no. 2, 2001, cf. in this issue i.a. Schmitt 2001 [1922], and Schmitt 2002 [1932]

(Schmitt 2001 [1922]: 29). That is how he starts a famous article from 1922 on the definition of sovereignty. The sovereign has two basic forms of existence: it is partly an institution, namely the state, the function of which i.a. is determined by the fact that it possesses a monopoly of force. And partly it is the will of the people, who appear in the shape of public opinion. In other words, the notion applies here that the will of the people is a kind of essence, a sum of individual wills, which in turn constitutes real sovereignty, the 'will' that lies under democracy. And he who has the capacity to identify this sovereignty may, under certain critical conditions, according to this understanding replace the will of the people.

What is the alternative? It is, I would assert, to replace the preference for an external player or cause by an internal player or cause, i.e. to turn one's gaze towards society's eigen-operations as an explanation of society. It is thereby possible to create a theoretical bulwark against the idea that the will of the people is a kind of essence, a sum of individual wills, which in turn constitutes the real sovereignty that lies under democracy. When society is not the sum of single individuals, then society's will is not the sum of individual wills. No, 'public opinion' is one of many different optics through which we observe phenomena in the outside world and communicate with each other.

Here, then, one finds an alternative to the fundamental question as to whether social order is possible or not. Social order is not created by the monarch via his regal power, the state via its power of the state or the people via its popular will moulding together the atoms of society to form a unity. No, social order is created by a diversity of communicative systems together creating an immensely complex and dynamic stability. Society does not exist by virtue of the purity of the social order but by virtue of the complex impurity of the social structures.

What does this example demonstrate? Firstly it demonstrates, how social science avoids reflecting its own unity. But secondly it demonstrates that at least one ought to avoid imagining that this reflection can be avoided. It can be determined that the sovereign is not an ontologically metaphysical instance, the 'player' or 'substance' that *ex machina* solves the description problem. Similarly, the 'network socie-ty' is not a metaphysical fact but a social self-description, i.e. a self-determining result of the eigen-operations of what is signified. Of course it is important to produce new results, collect new data and produce new theories. To recognise one's own limitation, to have an eye for the communicative tricks by which one resolves one's own dilemmas, is, however, equally important.

In Carl Schmitt, sovereignty was the 'secret' behind democracy. Is there also a 'secret' behind the network society to be found in Castells? Does he, in other words, operate with a metaphysical dis-tinction? It is not easy to answer that question, but a hint is found in the concept used by Castells that lies closest to what one could call a social metaphysics: The concept 'space of flows'. According to Castells, the 'space of flows' is the network society's alternative to the traditional societies' 'space of places' (Castells 1996: 378). In tradi-tional society, the organisational basic principle is the place: The meet-ing place, the place, the arena, the physically located mass-gathering. But in the network society, society's 'space of places' is supplemented by the networks' 'space of flows', which are defined as follows: 'The space of flow is the material organization of time-sharing social prac-tices that work through flows.' (Castells 1996: 412). In a certain sense, the concept can be interpreted as the form that social networks con-stitute and that they, on the other hand, are themselves formed of. If that is correct, 'space of flow' can be interpreted as the networks' form of meaning (see also Bo Kampmann Walther's article in this book).

The unit of distinction: the form of social science

It must be emphasised that I do not mean by the above that one can or ought to avoid empirical research and/or metaphysical categories. What would we do without the empirical distinction or the meta-physical concept? Nor do I mean that empirical or metaphysical state-ments are uninteresting. It is of course relevant to know whether 27% or 33% have access to the Internet. Carl Schmitt's identification of the sovereign has considerable phenomenological value.

It is just that it is insufficient. When the social researcher asks the question 'what is the case?', he does so as a researcher (and not as a journalist, politician or citizen), i.e. with the aim of saying something that can be claimed to be true. When he asks 'what lies behind it?', he once more does so as a researcher in a society that makes a distinction between politics and sovereignty possible, and that makes this distinction with the aim of identifying a cause, i.e. fulfilling the truth requirement on the basis of which the empirical distinction was made. So it is important that apart from asking and answering the two questions, i.e. making distinctions, one also considers what the unit of distinction is. What are the form prerequisites on which these distinctions are based? On the basis of what are these questions asked? What is the blind spot of social science or research?

This question can only be thematised if one observes the observer's way of making his observations, i.e. places oneself outside science and from such a vantage point observes its operations in a way that, as far as possible, makes science's operations the subject of outsider observations, i.e. adopts an anthropological view (this, for example, is Bruno Latour's project in his collection of articles *Pandora's Hope,* cf. Latour 1999).

According to a constructivist epistemology, every observation of the outside world takes place as the recognising system's construction of the outside world via this system's own blind spot. Just as the eye is blind at the point of the eyeball to which the optic nerve is attached, so is every observation of the world determined by a difference being made: A difference between the signified and the non-signified aspect. The difference that is used in the observation operation cannot in itself be observed by the observation. It constitutes the observer's blind spot. It is, as Luhmann (Luhmann 1990) says with a reference to Michel Serres, not the *subject* of the observation but the 'parasite' of the observation (Serres 1980). One could also – using an expression I have from Dirk Baecker, who in turn has taken it from Serres – call it the 'joker' of the observation (Baecker 2000).

When the ontologist – still using Luhmann's examples – demonstrates what 'is' and is not, then his blind spot is the difference between being and non-being. When the empiricist demonstrates what are facts and what are interpretations, then this very distinction between facts and interpretations is a blind spot. His distinction implies that one can first observe and then interpret. When the moralist demonstrates what is good, his blind spot is the difference between the good and the bad. His distinction is based on sure and indisputable knowledge as to what is good, and should he come to doubt this, he must invoke a universal guarantee for 'the good', as certain clergymen do: Claim that there is no society without an ethic, and that ethics are God's work.

Both the ontologist and the moralist do not therefore simply talk about the world but also about what they do not know. In other words, they are sure of a case about whose uncertainty they are unknowing. They observe the world and pronounce on their observation via their blind spot. And if anyone pronounces on the blindness of others, the latter will react with anger or silence, because any system that is irritated by a disturbance that the system cannot use to construct an eigen-complexity will react with systematic closure, i.e. rejection. If someone suggests that the observation of the chosen phenomenon must also be observed, the ontologist reacts with irritation or irony. For he has never heard of anything as futile and superfluous – he who only observes what is the case.

This does not mean that one is at the mercy of one's eigen-optic. It is perfectly possible to have a close look, so to speak, at the parasite, the joker, the blind spot – by shifting one's point of observation. The person who observes empirical research as an observation operation naturally does not claim that 'reality' does not exist. On the contrary. 'Who believes more in the objectivity of science than those who claim that it can be turned into an object of inquiry?' Latour rhetorically asks (Latour 1999: 3). But it does mean that the observation also must be observed. There are no absolute alternatives. There is no 'truth' as opposed to 'false consciousness'; 'critical research' is not in any absolute sense 'better' than positivist research. The question of better versus worse research is not decided by a moral distinction between an 'affirmative' and a 'critical' position. On the other hand, the problem is not solved by a self-ironic shrug of the shoulders. One cannot get rid of these problems by treating the empirical method pragmatically: Which case lies closest? Which phenomenon is most 'exemplary'? But when these distinctions are proposed, they must also be subject to critical observation.

The 'network society': A point of observation

One of the questions that one hereby seeks to answer is that of which position of observation is appropriate, and to define for what it is appropriate. In the present case, it is a question of finding out what it means that one observes society through the optic that calls society a 'network society', and of placing oneself outside or next to this point of observation, i.e. to observe the observer. How can we get at an understanding of 'the network society' as a social self-description category?

We can do so, for example, by calling society something else. Only by doing this can – once more – a distinction be created that makes observation possible, namely the observation of the 'network society' as a socio-semantic category.

That is why in the following I intend to subject the concept the 'network society' to a critical evaluation. I want, so to speak, to try to arrive at a conceptual distance from the network society and observe the observation of it – as a network society. That is also why I wish to advance an alternative conceptual approach, namely via the concept of complexity.

It therefore does not mean that I will arrive at the truth about society. But it does mean that I can make my observations, and that I can make explicit the premises for these observations, so others can also observe my blind spot. It is a question of being able to lead with the joker so that others are forced to reveal their cards. After that, however, the game is not over. But the next round can begin.

Critique of Castells' network concept as a sociological concept

Castells' network concept

What is a so-called 'network society'? The concept was introduced by Manuel Castells in his colossal three-volume work, since when it has given its name to books, government strategies and research programmes. Towards the end of the first volume he writes: 'Networks constitute the new social morphology of our societies, and the diffusion of networking logic substantially modifies the operation and outcomes in processes of production, experience, power, and culture' (Castells 1996: 469).

In his article 'Materials for an exploratory theory of the network society' (Castells 2000) Castells further develops the concept of network and network society as a special form – as he had already written in *The Rise of the Network Society* – of 'social morphology': 'A network is a set of interconnected nodes. A node is the point where the curve intersects itself.' Somewhat surprisingly – considering the fact that what he introduces should ostensibly be a new concept – he adds: 'Networks are very old forms of social organization' (Castells 2000: 15, cf. also Castells 1996: 470).

Here, Castells is building on a rich sociological tradition. There are obvious connections that go back to Tönnies' classic distinction between Gemeinschaft and Gesellschaft, and there is a clear relationship to Georg Simmel's answer from 1908 to sociology's standard question: 'Wie ist Gesellschaft möglich?' 'In order to avoid to the greatest possible extent a dispute about definitions, I wish to base myself on the broadest possible conception of society: that it exists where several individuals reciprocally interact,' Simmel wrote (Simmel 1908: 24). This means that practically 'everything' can be termed a society: '[...] from a brief reunion with the family on a walk, from all relations that can be 'terminated', to interdependence with a state, from fleeting contact at a hotel party to the close solidarity of a medieval guild' (Ibid.).

Castells compares the network form with other forms of social morphology, e.g. centralised hierarchies, emphasising that on the one hand it has advantages in the form of flexibility and adaptability, but on the other hand has disadvantages, because it is not good at coordinating activities or at handling '[...] the complexity of a given task beyond a certain size of the network.' (Ibid.)[6]

Even so, the network has, according to Castells, enjoyed a renaissance as a social morphology. The cause of this Castells finds in the new information and communication technologies. Network-based forms of organisation '[...] have taken on a new life in the Information Age by becoming information networks, powered by new information technologies' (Ibid.).

Castells' explanation for the renaissance of the network form is that the new information technologies solve the problems that formerly characterised this form. 'For the first time, the introduction of new information/communication technologies allows networks to keep their flexibility and adaptability, thus asserting their evolutionary nature.

While, at the same time, these technologies allow for co-ordination and management of complexity, in an interactive system which features feedback effects, and communication patterns from everywhere to everywhere within the network. It follows an unprecedented combination of flexibility and task implementation, of co-ordinated decision making, and decentralized execution, which provide a superior social morphology for all human action' (Ibid.).

That modern society has the form of a network society has, according to Castells, innumerable consequences and forms of expression.

It changes the concept of 'social distance', since social distance now depends on membership of networks rather than physical and geographical distance. Not only is the distance between two points shorter if they belong to the same network than if they do not do so. Physical, social, economic, political and cultural distance '[...] for a

---

6   Unlike Finnemann (2003), Castells does not, in other words, want to characterise hierarchies etc. as 'networks'.

given point varies between zero (for any point in the same network) and infinite (for any point external to the network)' (Castells 1996: 470).

It changes the relation between social inclusion and exclusion. 'The inclusion/exclusion in networks, and the architecture of relationships between networks, enacted by light-speed operating information technologies, configurate dominant processes and functions in our societies' (Ibid.).

Hereby it also dramatically influences the power relationships in society: '[...] the network morphology is [...] a source of dramatic reorganization of power relationships. Switches connecting the networks [...] are the privileged instruments of power. Thus, the switchers are the power holders' (Ibid.: 471).

Indeed, even the man-nature relationship seems to change character. From having originally been a nature-man relationship where nature dominated the relationship, via the man-nature relationship of industrial society, where man was the dominating entity, we are now entering a relationship that must be termed culture-culture, because nature is an artificial phenomenon, i.e. a phenomenon that exists by virtue of man's technological efforts (Ibid.: 477). In other words, nature has also become a point in the network.

Provisionally summing up, network society represents, according to Castells, a return of the network as a social morphology, but in a version that maintains the advantages and eliminates the disadvantages. The cause is the new information and communication technologies which, thanks to almost unlimited feedback potential on a previously unseen scale can combine flexibility and coordination: The result – and here I am repeating Castells' praise of this step forward – is a '[...] superior social morphology for all human action.' Here, Castells would seem to be close to positions found in, for example, Negroponte (1995) and Dertouzos (1997), cf. my critique in the book *The Hypercomplex Society* (Qvortrup 2003). On the one hand, present-day society – thanks to the new information and communication technologies – is characterised by everyone potentially being in communicative contact with everyone else. This creates a colossal problem of complexity. On the other hand, the same new information and communication technologies can solve this problem by virtue of their information handling potential.[7]

Objections to Castells' network concept

I disagree with Castells regarding his view of the consequences of information and communication technologies for society. In my opinion, it is unrealistic to claim that the new information and communication technologies, thanks to their communicative range and feedback possibilities, can be used – to use Simmel's expression – to make a society possible whose immense complexity is, among other things, due to the global communicative range of the same technologies. To regard the relation between society and technology as one between problem and solution is to separate an analysis of society and that of technology in a way that is highly surprising for a sociologist. The consequence is a sociological 'under-determination' of technology.

In addition, however, the way Castells uses the network concept means that it appears to be a concept that in itself is loaded with a theoretical deficiency. The distance between the theoretical conceptualisation and the empirical analyses in Castells is too great. The question is whether the concept of modern society as a 'network society', i.e. – to use Simmel's expression – with 'the broadest possible notion of society' is valid as an epochal definition. My reply is that it is not.

---

7   This does not mean I am saying that there are not many interesting and relevant observations in his three volumes on the network society. I am merely trying to identify Castells' point of observation and the 'format' via which he observes modern society. And here I believe that my characterisation does justice to Castells' project. Just look at his own summary of the project in volume three of the work: 'The information technology revolution induced the emergence of informationalism, as the material foundation of a new society. Under informationalism, the generation of wealth, the exercise of power, and the creation of cultural codes came to depend on the technological capacity of societies and individuals, with information technology as the core of this capacity. Information technology became the indispensable tool for the effective implementation processes of socio-economic restructuring. Particularly important was its role in allowing the development of networking as a dynamic, self-expanding form of organization of human activity. This prevailing, networking logic transforms all domains of social and economic life' (Castells 1998: 336).

But what then can the concept 'network society' be used for? What lies in it that can be built on, if one's interest is in an epochal identification? Concealed in the question is the assumption that the concept is not a chance and either obtuse or consciously misleading concept, but that as a socio-semantic phenomenon it contains a significance that ought to be taken seriously.

The core statement of the concept is that every point in modern society (I am here and in the rest of the article using this concept as a neutral definition, i.e. as a non-definition, for the 'social morphology' that Castells and many other people seek to demarcate) is potentially speaking communicatively linked to any other point.

This means that for me Castells has at least implicitly referred to a core issue concerning modern society, namely its immense communicative complexity. He opens for what could be called a second point of observation, the appropriateness of which I will argue in favour of. That there is an immediate linking potential between all points in a given set implies an immense complexity or – to use Shannon's concept of information – an immense amount of information. But if the number of links between nodes in a network is unlimited, it is not an ordered but a chaotic network. So society is thereby only characterised negatively. For the concept network expresses the immense complexity loading of modern society (no matter whether it is measured spatially, as for example by Anthony Giddens, or temporally as by Virilio), but it does not provide any insight into how this complexity loading is handled – something else, then, than this problem is solved by the *deus ex machina* of the new information and communication technologies. So one could say that in reality the concept expresses the impossibility of modern society rather than justifies its quite evident possibility empirically speaking. To conceptualise the network society as a global interaction system – i.e. as a society that on the one hand is global in its communicative range but on the other hand is left to interaction's limited agents of observation and feedback, i.e. to the double contingency of immediate communication (and that is really what Castells is doing) – does not help us understand the *sui generis* of this social morphology.

From the network to the complexity paradigm

Complexity loading

If my criticism of Castells is correct, there are two possibilities. One is to deny that 'anything new' is taking place, i.e. to adopt the view that there is no need to identify any specific, new social morphology. The other is to endorse the idea that something new *is* taking place, but that this new feature is not satisfactorily categorised by Castells. Here (as I have done in Lars Qvortrup 1998, 2001, 2003 and 2004) I choose the latter possibility.

The essential thing about the network concept, as mentioned, is that modern society is characterised in principle by all actions being potentially communicatively accessible. The consequence of this is an immense complexity loading.

This loading can be expressed spatially: There is always access to a surplus of linking possibilities. Perhaps this has 'always' been so, but under the conditions that Castells depicts this is an experience-based relation. We know that this is how things are. We know that we do not know what we do not know. Which means: We know that there are things that, technically speaking, we could know, but that for reasons of capacity we must actively or passively deselect.

But complexity loading can also be expressed in terms of time. The next state of the network is in principle unpredictable or, to use Shannon's expression: since the probability of the next state of the social system is infinitely small, the amount of information required to know the next state is infinitely large. It was this condition that Herbert A. Simon expressed by the concept 'bounded rationality': That we know that we never know enough. That belief in the rational choice of the next state is illusory.

In that sense the concept of what Castells calls the network society is not utopian but dystopian. The modernity-based expectation of a rational form of society, whether it be market-based, welfare state-like or socialist, is no longer a realistic expectation but an illusion. And this is also the case even though the answer is not social constructions but technological ones. Nor can digital information and communication technologies neutralise this immense complexity loading.

So there is no answer that 'solves' the problem. But there are counter-moves that contribute with temporary stabilisings. My proposal is that the formula for these temporary stabilisings is, as Luhmann has said, that only complexity can reduce complexity (Luhmann 1995: 26), i.e. that the growth in communicative linking possibilities (no matter whether they are due to world trade, global media systems, digital networks or other phenomena) must be accompanied by a corresponding construction of social inner complexity (and when I write 'must' it is not meant normatively but only in respect of the observation that this society actually maintains itself).

The 'social morphology' of complexity

The complexity-theoretical logic – the 'social morphology' – on which this paradigm is based can be summarised as follows:

A cohesive set of elements is termed complex when each element because of immanent limitations in the linking capacity of the elements cannot at any time be connected to every other element (cf. Luhmann 1995: 24). It should be noted here that 'complexity' is not defined as an absolute but as a relative concept. Whether a set or a system can be termed complex depends not only on the number of connective possibilities, i.e. what one could call outer complexity, but also on the 'connective capacity', which in turn is an expression of their inner complexity.

Complexity – i.e. a surplus of connective possibilities – produces enforced selection. The individual element must, in order to constitute a system, choose one or more connection from the total number of possibilities. This enforced selection results in turn in contingency, i.e. a knowledge that something has been selected while something else – which might just as easily have been selected – has been deselected. An expression of the contingency of a social system is therefore risk, since risk can be defined as conscious or self-induced danger. One cannot 'run' a danger, but one can run a risk. A point here is that an increasing number of phenomena that would formerly have been labelled dangers now appear to be risks, because they are the result of a choice. Cancer is a risk, because in principle we could have avoided it by taking prophylactic measures. Traffic accidents are a risk, because we could have improved traffic safety. Indeed, even death is tendentially seen as a risk, because we could have guarded ourselves against it.

While such a selection-strategic procedure could formerly have led to an expectation of risk-neutralisation, because one expected all the right links could be selected and all the wrong ones deselected – this was an expectation of rational solutions – the awareness that enforced coercion involves contingency means that this rationalist optimism is no longer capable of being realised. The perspective is not an expectation that it is possible to create an absolute complexity-handling surplus, but that there will always be a surplus of possibilities. For the higher our linking capacity, the more elements will potentially be capable of being linked. The more one knows, the more one knows that one does not know.

This means finally that the elements pay increasing attention to their own linking capacity: The eigen-complexity of the elements is activated, among other things, in an observation of their eigen-complexity. The consequence of this is hypercomplexity: 'A system that orientates itself towards its own complexity and that seeks to understand it as complexity we refer to as hypercomplex' (Luhmann 1995: 471; cf. also Qvortrup 1998, 2001 and 2003). So 'hypercomplexity' is not defined as a common sense term as 'an enormous amount of complexity' but in very precise terms as a concept for second order complexity: Hypercomplexity is complexity applied to complexity.

If this is assumed to be the basic conditions for a system that operates on the basis of there being a surplus of linking possibilities, one can identify two basic strategies the aim of which is to handle complexity – namely exclusion and inclusion. Both of these strategies have implicit potential problems.

An exclusion strategy seeks to deselect linking possibilities. It strives for simplification. The consequence is risk production, because what is excluded is beyond reach and thus cannot be controlled. An inclusion strategy seeks to increase the number of linking possibilities by raising the linking capacity of the system. The system changes its immanent limitations by increasing its inner complexity. The consequence is, however, that this building up of inner complexity may in itself lead to a new, but transformed, complexity problem.

A good example of the latter is the new information and communication technologies. On the one hand, they raise the linking capacity of the social system and therefore help to deal with complexity. On the other hand, they thereby increase the inner complexity of the system and produce a complexity problem. So the Internet therefore does not – as some critics of technology believe – represent a problem, but nor does it – as some technology optimists believe – represent an answer. It represents a dilemma, because it raises the complexity management capacity of a system, however simultaneously creating the new complexity problem of managing the complexity of the Internet. While the network society paradigm assumes that ICTs are answers to social problems, the hypercomplexity society paradigm assumes that ICT is an answer to problems, but an answer that produces new problems. Thus, the complexity-theoretical paradigm can thereby see things that the network paradigm cannot see. What the complexity paradigm cannot see, others must point out from another point of observation.

Knowledge and complexity

'Only complexity can reduce complexity,' Niklas Luhmann writes in *Soziale Systeme* (Luhmann 1995: 26). In terms of distinctions, the formula can be expressed as a relation between inner and outer complexity.

But how can one define inner complexity in meaning-based, i.e. mental and social systems? My proposal is to define inner complexity as knowledge. It is by producing knowledge that mental and social systems handle outside-world complexity.

69

Why? Because the function of knowledge is to restrict the expectation horizon, i.e. the number of possible future events. I know that the hotplate is hot when it is turned on, which is why I do not place my hand on it. The organisation knows that if prices are increased, sales decrease. The researcher knows – or thought he knew – that all swans are white and thus does not expect to find a black swan.

This does not assume that knowledge is the same as secure knowledge. It is possible that modern hotplates will be developed which are hot only when in contact with pots and pans but not when in contact with hands and other organic material. It cannot be excluded that increased prices under certain circumstances will increase and not decrease sales. It has transpired that certain black birds can according to all other criteria be classified as swans. In all cases we are dealing with learning, and learning results in modified expectation horizons and therefore in new knowledge.

The consequence of this is that it is inappropriate – or at least insufficient – to observe a modern society as a network society, for social or medial networks do not of themselves make society possible. It can, though, be meaningful to observe society as a *knowing* society, for knowledge reduces complexity and makes society possible. But knowledge both has to be linked to a complex outside world and knowledge also exists in various configurations. The former – the structural linking of knowledge and world – presupposes medial networks. The latter – knowledge configurations – can be used to characterise network configurations.

Critique of Castells' concept of knowledge

In most theories of the knowledge society, any explicit, sociologically relevant definition of knowledge is absent. As early as 1959, the English economist and organization analyst Edith Penrose emphasized the growing importance of knowledge in economy, but in addition she admitted that the whole subject of knowledge is so 'slippery' that it is impossible to get a firm grip of it (Penrose 1959: 77). In 1969, Peter Drucker announced that knowledge had become the central capital, cost centre and basic resource of the economy (Drucker 1969: ix).

However, he still did not suggest how to appropriately define this basic resource. Approximately thirty years later, Luhmann correctly summarised: '[…] was ist Wissen? Wenn man von der Gesellschafts-theorie ausgeht und selbst wenn man die moderne Gesellschaft als "Wissensgesellschaft" bezeichnet, findet man keinen brauchbaren Begriff des Wissens' (Luhmann 2002: 97).

Sometimes knowledge is defined as an essence or substance, cf. for instance the OECD report from 2004, *Innovation in the Knowledge Economy*, which focuses on 'implications for education and learning'. Here, it is emphasised that it is important to have a clear idea of '[…] what it is that is passing through the electronic pipelines: knowledge, information or data?' (OECD 2004: 18). However, the challenges of education and learning – why doesn't teaching automatically lead to adequate learning, if teaching is only a matter of transporting knowledge? – and of knowledge sharing – why is knowledge sharing actually most often *not* happening automatically? – cannot be answered if it is assumed that knowledge is a substance that can easily be transported from one person to the other. It is well known that this is *not* what happens in the classroom or in the knowledge sharing organisation. Knowledge about something is a representation of something according to interpretation standards, which may change from person to person and from teacher to pupil. My knowledge is not equal to your knowledge, and thus it is a simplification to assume that it can just like that be transferred from me to you.

In other contexts, knowledge has been defined in a restricted way as certified knowledge. In his classic book about post-industrial society Daniel Bell defined knowledge as '[…] a set of organized statements of facts or ideas, presenting a reasoned judgment or an experimental result, which is transmitted to others through some communication medium is some systematic form' (Bell 1973: 175). In his book about the network society, Castells has, as he says, 'no compelling reason to improve on' this definition (Castells 1996: 17). But certified knowledge is only one aspect of knowledge, as for instance Michael Polanyi has convincingly argued. Also, tacit knowledge – the knowledge of e.g. how to ride a bike – is knowledge, although it cannot be written down or 'proved' and certified in any traditional scientific way.

The main problem, however, is that knowledge is defined without any context. Not only do Bell and Castells claim that context-free, i.e. objectivised, knowledge *exists*; knowledge is simply *defined* as 'certified', i.e. decontextualised. The prerequisite for something being knowledge is – no matter what – that it exists independently of the person that knows something. This makes the theory unable to understand the many problems to do with knowledge, namely that knowledge cannot simply be acquired in the same way as one drinks milk, and that without problems being involved it cannot be shared like a plot of land, a layer cake or a fortune. Secondly, the theory cannot account for the existence of so many forms of knowledge and new knowledge. One form of new knowledge is the constant accumulation of factual knowledge, of facts. Formerly, we knew that nine planets orbited the sun. Now we know that – depending on our definition – there are ten. A second form of new knowledge, however, is the one that presupposes that the very structure of knowledge changes. Formerly, one knew that the earth was the centre of the universe. Now one knows that the universe does not have a centre. Thirdly and finally, a substantivist definition of knowledge presupposes that there is an inverse proportionality between knowledge and non-knowledge. The more we know, the less we do not know. But experience tells us that more knowledge does not create less non-knowledge. The converse is true: More knowledge creates to an over-proportional extent more non-knowledge. The more we know, the more we know that we do not know (cf. Luhmann 1997: 1106).

So there are reasons to look around for a more functional definition of knowledge.

What is knowledge?

What is knowledge? The question sounds simple, but the answer is difficult. It has occupied people's minds ever since the first philosophical questions were formulated.

Right now, I am looking out of the window at the snow melting and at the fir trees with their dripping branches. But how do I know that what I am looking at are trees, and that what covers the ground is snow?

If one asks the snow, it does not know that it is snow, and the tree hardly has sufficient self-awareness to observe itself as something with a name. It does not stand straight and tall, even though I am sitting inside here praising its tree-ness. The knowledge we have of the world is thus a knowledge that we have created.

From a phenomenological point of view, knowledge is a concept of sure expectations. I know, i.e. I can remember and agree with others, that the denotation of the thing outside the window that has precisely that shape and those colours is: Fir tree. I know that hotplates can indeed be hot, and that doors are hard if one does not open them before passing through. I know that the neighbour buys breakfast rolls at the baker's every day at 7am. Those who believe know that God created the world. Well, maybe they have not made that observation themselves, but they trust others who say that that is the way it is. A workman knows how to use an electric screwdriver and a saw. In the 15th century, people knew that the earth was the centre of the universe. And my bank adviser knows how to stretch money.

Based on the above, I would define knowledge as *observations that have been confirmed over time*. That is also how Niklas Luhmann defines knowledge: 'als Kondensierung von Beobachtungen' (Luhmann 1990a: 123).

This means that knowledge and true knowledge represent two different phenomena. True knowledge is a special case of knowledge. The general concept of knowledge '[...] bezieht auch und vor allem alltägliches Verhalten ein, das nicht im Hinblick auf Wissenschaftlichkeit, ja nicht einmal im Hinblick auf wahr und unwahr beobachtet wird' (Ibid.).

One of the results of the development of a modern society – a development that has been particularly observable in European societies – is, however, that various forms of knowledge have developed – each of which is connected to a specific function system. Scientific knowledge has developed into being *cognitively* stylised meaning with very high and highly formalised demands concerning the condensation of observations, i.e. into knowledge of the relation between true and non-true knowledge, while legal knowledge is the result of *normatively* stylised knowledge of the relation between right and wrong (ibid.: 138). In comparison, religious knowledge can be defined as theologically stylised and highly ritualised knowledge of the relation between immanence and transcendence.

Forms of knowledge

Above, I defined knowledge as observations that had been confirmed over time or in a social community. We have also seen that there are various types of knowledge. But knowledge also exists at various levels. This is what I call forms of knowledge.

The explanation is the following: One does not only observe the world around one. One also observes oneself when making one's observations. I look at the snow. But when I look at it I start to think about clearing the pavement. This is linked to a second form of knowledge. We look at the fir tree and start to discuss how we happen to agree that it actually is a tree. 'What is that in the corner of the garden: Is it a tree, or just a bush?' Or if our grandchild was in a creative mood – or perhaps was a little older – she might point at the snow and say: 'Just think if it was sugar! Or diamonds! Just think how rich we'd be!' She has reached a philosophical age and begun to develop a third form of knowledge.

The point is that we not only look at the world and create knowledge from it. We also observe the way which we look at the world, i.e. we make what could be referred to as a second order observation – an observation of the observation. And our philosophical grandchild takes a further step: She observes the criteria for our observations. She makes observations of the third order.

To illustrate the system of forms of knowledge let us use a very simple example: A perfectly ordinary hammer. What do we know about it?

Firstly, we know *what* a hammer is. We have ready knowledge or, as we will refer to it, qualifications. We know what a hammer looks like. We know where Oslo lies. We know which German prepositions take the dative. We know it was Christian IV who built the Danish Stock Exchange. This knowledge we call *first order knowledge*. It is knowledge results from a simple or registering observation of the world around us.

Secondly, we know *how* to use a hammer. We can use it for driving in nails. We have competences, i.e. we can use our knowledge to solve tasks. With the aid of our knowledge of German prepositions we can answer the question: Where is the nearest post office? 'Unter dem Linden,' we proudly answer. This knowledge we call *second order knowledge*. It is knowledge that results from our not simply observing phenomena in the world around us but also observing our observation of these phenomena. Someone asks us to drive in a nail. We then retrieve our knowledge of what a hammer is and how it is used. We observe the hammer, so to speak, through the task of the nail to be driven into the wall. In the scientific world one speaks of methods, for methods do not have to do with the world but with how we look at the world. Have you used qualitative or quantitive methods, one asks. What one is now doing is observing observations.

Thirdly, we know *why* we call what we see a hammer. Implements can be divided into categories: Screwdrivers, hammers, saws, etc. We are now undertaking not simply a second order observation but a third order one. We are, so to speak, looking at the criteria for the way which we make observations. What causes us to call the object in the photo a hammer? When one makes use of this form of knowledge, it is possible to be creative. For now one can change the criteria for what one knows. A hammer may perhaps not only be characterised as a wooden shaft with a metal head but as an implement to drive sharp objects into walls with. Once one has asked this question, one can invent new hammers, i.e. new implements for driving in nails. One is no longer bound by a narrow definition of a hammer. In the scientific world one would now speak of theories. If one views the world via a theory, the world looks one way. If one views the world via another theory, the world looks different. Some of us can probably recall history teaching in the 1970s. 'Now was it Christian IV who built the

Danish Stock Exchange?' 'Wasn't it the workers who did that, i.e. those who for a pittance he forced to slave away for him?' When one asks that kind of question, i.e. launches new theories or paradigms, the world suddenly looks different. We know this not only from science but from art: After having seen the film 'The Birds' by Alfred Hitchcock, crows and gulls no longer look the way they did before.

Fourthly and finally, we know that the hammer, along with the other implements and those who use them, are part of a tool and workshop culture. We know *for whom and with whom* we know what we know. All our knowledge constitutes a common knowledge culture, where the one type of knowledge determines the other. If we pool all our knowledge, we can almost make out the contours of a boundary: The boundary to what we do not know and perhaps *cannot ever know*. This fourth order knowledge is probably the one it is most difficult to understand and to describe. A theorist who has inspired me in thinking of these forms of knowledge – the American Gregory Bateson – once described it as a knowledge we do not have individually but one that is the result of a collective evolution. We know it from the common tool culture. Or we know it in organisations and companies as what is called 'basic assumptions', i.e. the way in which one knows everything one knows. A way that it is hard to think out of, or place oneself outside of. Sometimes, in order to illustrate this fourth form of knowledge, one uses religious images: God, one says, is the one who knows what we cannot know.

Table 2.1: Categories of Knowledge

Form of knowledge	Knowledge systematics	Knowledge term
1st order knowledge: Factual knowledge	Knowledge of the outside world	Qualifications
2nd order knowledge: Situative knowledge	Knowledge about knowledge	Competences
3rd order knowledge: Systemic knowledge	Knowledge about the knowledge system	Creativity
4th order knowledge: World knowledge	Total, collective knowledge	Culture

Knowledge and network morphology

Formerly, indeed, until quite recently, knowledge was thought of as an extended field that admittedly grew and grew, but which did so from a centre and that also hereby approached the boundary of possible knowledge. Therefore the concept of all knowledge – the 'encyclopedia' – is derived from the word 'circle', i.e. the form that is defined as having a centre. Similarly, the institution where new knowledge is produced is still referred to as a 'university' and not a 'multiversity', i.e. the place where one's gaze is in one direction, toward the source of all knowledge.

Today, though, according to Michel Serres, we know that knowledge does not have a fixed order and a centre, but that knowledge arises and exists by virtue of its '[...] momentum, the energy in its motion' (Serres 1997: 38). We know that the person who believes himself to be standing at the centre of knowledge is blind, for he cannot see what he cannot see. 'The person who considers himself perfect can neither see or feel a limit and therefore does not understand the ardent need to transcend an inaccessible boundary, whose position he is uncertain about' (Serres 1997: 16).

The consequence is that digital networks can not only be conceived as transport systems that, according to various principles, since they are capable of linking the individual nodes in the networks, can ensure the best possible transportation and distribution of certified knowledge. No, it is also possible to identify a structural relationship between forms of knowledge and forms of network.

Knowledge of the first order is created and exchanged via simple point-to-point networks. Factual knowledge or 'object-knowledge' of the one network node can be passed on to the second node via a simple transfer-relation between the two nodes; similarly, first order knowledge can be distributed in organisations via hierarchical one-way networks.

Second order knowledge is defined as knowledge about knowledge, for example, as knowledge concerning the ability to use factual knowledge for problem-solving purposes. Here, one not only has to know something but possess a methodic knowledge, i.e. a knowledge of how the object knowledge in question is to be used. To be able to create and exchange second order knowledge it is therefore necessary to establish a recursive relation between transfer and code or, in network terminology, between network transfer and network protocol.

Third order knowledge is defined as knowledge about knowledge about knowledge. For example, knowledge of the way in which the relation between object-knowledge and problem-solving knowledge is conditioned. Third order knowledge is knowledge about how codes – or in knowledge terminology: methods – are conditioned. In functionalist organisation theory one speaks of 'basic assumptions' (cf. Schein), i.e. what one does not know that one knows. In sociological terminology, third order knowledge is based on the distinction between codes and social system; in Castells' terminology we are dealing with the distinction between protocol and space of flows.

Finally, fourth order knowledge is defined as the totality of world knowledge: all that can be known. In Castell's terminology this would refer to the – invisible – distinction between networks and non-networks, i.e. the transcendental conditions for networks.

Table 2.2: Knowledge-based Network Morphologies

Knowledge Category	Network Category	Communication/observation category
1st order knowledge	Simple point-to-point coupling	Transfer/non-transfer – simple observation as indication/distinction
2nd order	Network/protocol	Transfer/code – the recursive observation, or the observation of codes as a precondition for transfer
3rd order	Protocol/space of flows	Code/social system – the observation of the emergence of codes through the operation of a social system
4th order	Network/ non-network	Society/transcendentality – the observation of society from a position outside society (the transcendental observer)

Social strategies for dealing with complexity

My assertion is that in the above-described continuous building-up of inner and outer complexity one finds an important source of the social morphology of modern society. I would like to mention some examples of this interaction between the development of outer complexity and the building-up of inner complexity in attempting to exemplify the relation between inner and outer complexity at the social and organisational as well as the individual level.

Functional differentiation

My first and perhaps most obvious example is that growth in the extent of possible communicative couplings is accompanied by a growing functional differentiation – indeed, that the functional differentiation as described by Niklas Luhmann seems to be a possible model of a complexity-based social morphology of modern society.

According to Luhmann, one can identify the following ideal-typical differentiation morphologies which precede – but also exist side by side with – the predominant functional differentiation of our age (cf. Luhmann 1997: 613):

- segmental differentiation
- centre-periphery differentiation, or horizontal in- and exclusion
- stratificatory differentiation, or vertical in- and exclusion

The first type, i.e. segmentary differentiation, is characterised by each single, undifferentiated social system being based on reciprocal observation among those present. A social 'segment' maintains itself by virtue of reciprocal observations. It is, to use Castells' concept, a simple network, a system of reciprocally interconnected elements. In Luhmann's terminology it would be called an interaction system.

It seems to be generally believed that present-day society represents a return to segmentary differentiation, but this time not in the form of spatially limited social segments, but in the form of a global interaction system – only now, so to speak, made possible through the use of digital information and communication technologies. This would seem to be Castells' perception.

His point of departure is the completely correct one that interaction systems have very clear, narrow boundaries regarding their capacity to maintain eigen-stability. It is not possible to maintain stability in large social systems if the only available means is reciprocal observation of individual actors or network nodes. However, it seems to be assumed that the new information and communication technologies, are able to solve this problem.

As already mentioned, Castells is far from being alone here. On the contrary, this characterisation of modern society has been used by a long line of theorists, although very few of them indeed have had such high sociological ambitions as Castells. There are many people who characterise present-day society as a 'global village' (McLuhan) or a 'global information marketplace' (Dertouzos 1997), and who thus – as Steven G. Jones pointed out in 1998 – focus on similarities between global 'cyberspace' and former tribal societies, village communes, marketplaces and squares, etc., since they celebrate the apparent return to Tönnies' 'Gemeinschaft' (Jones 1998: 21).

In relation to this, Luhmann stresses the difference between a segmentarily differentiated society of loosely linked interaction systems and present-day society. With the potential global communication between people who are virtually present in a common time and a common space, the problem concerning the handling of complexity increases on a corresponding scale, quite simply because the tools for handling complexity in basic face-to-face communication are relatively limited. It is well-known that in the communication that takes place in interaction groups there are many inclusion and exclusion functions, functions related to the identification of explicit and implicit communication roles and patterns, etc. Even if these tools work well in relation to the structural stabilisation of small interaction groups, they are nevertheless not particularly effective when it comes to the stabilisation, maintenance and continuation of large – indeed global – social groups and systems.

According to Luhmann, it is not possible to gain any sufficient conceptual advantage from referring to present-day modernity as a return to a – now global – 'Gemeinschaft'. On the contrary. Even from a conceptual point of view, one must, in relation to present-day global society '[...] bid farewell to all Gemeinschaft mythologies – more precisely, we relegate them to the level of self-description of social systems' (Luhmann 1995: 220).

With regard to Castells' concept of modern society as a network society based on information technology, Luhmann emphasises functional differentiation as – to use Castells' concept – the predominant social morphology of our time. Functional differentiation differs from all previous forms of social differentiation by not being divalent but polyvalent. It does not operate with one distinction criterion but with in principle an infinite number of distinction criteria in a society. For precisely this reason, it is an example of a society that is characterised by, in principle, global communicative range – and thereby enormous outer complexity – developing a corresponding inner complexity.

Every functionally differentiated subsystem is characterised by operating on the basis of its specific 'Leitdifferenz', i.e. basic distinction, its symbolically generalised media, its predominant code and its form of reflection.[8] This means that the system of functionally differentiated subsystems represents both the inclusion and exclusion strategy.

They function inclusively, because together they contribute to the building-up of very considerable inner complexity in society. 'Eine solche Entwicklung steigert die Komplexität des Gesellschaftssystems,' Luhmann asserts (Luhmann 1997: 616). But it does mean that mechanisms develop at the same time that can handle this growing inner complexity. 'Entsprechend müssen evolutionäre Errungenschaften vorgegeben sein oder nachentwickelt werden, die höhere Komplexität reduzieren können: so Schrift, Geldwesen, bürokratische Organisation, um nur einige Beispiele zu nennen.' (Luhmann 1997: 616).

The consequence is a double effect of, on the one hand, a very con-

---

8   This naturally does not mean that a player in a particular function system cannot operate on the basis of various different 'Leitdifferenzen'. On the contrary, individuals in a modern society are precisely not bound by a particular social positioning but can operate freely among function systems as a 'homo viator'.

siderable dynamic stability and, on the other hand, a just as considerable 'inner irritability': Such a society '[...] hat in der Autopoiesis ihre Funktionssysteme zwar eine Stabilität ohnegleichen [...]. Zugleich ist sie aber auch in einem Maße durch sich selbst irritierbar wie keine Gesellschaft zuvor' (Luhmann 1997: 618).

Each of these subsystems, however, functions exclusively, because they undertake couplings with the outside world via a single coupling criterion. The economic system function via the criterion of payment/non-payment; the scientific system via the criterion of truth/non-truth; the religious system via the criterion of transcendence/immanence; the political system via the criterion of power/-non-power. This is their strength but also their weakness. They cannot of themselves include other criteria. This, however, organisations are capable of doing. Companies can include ethical or ecological criteria and thus alongside financial accounts also keep ethical or green accounts. Universities can supplement true/false codings with ethical considerations. By means of this, they raise their coupling capacity. But at the same time they reduce their decision-making competence.

Organisational strategies for the handling of complexity: Structural coupling

One characteristic of the social morphology of modern society is functional differentiation. A second characteristic is boundary crossing and structural couplings between various, reciprocally differentiated social systems and between organisations and their surroundings. Here too there is a potential for handling complexity.

One of the terms for this phenomenon is Karl Weick's 'boundary crossing', i.e. the fact that organisation systems use various fields of knowledge that interact and counteract with each other in order to build up inner complexity. Wenger, McDermott and Snyder are, in my opinion, right in claiming that the boundary concept ought to be liberated from its usual negative connotation (Wenger, McDermott and Snyder 2002: 153). Not only is the combination of traditionally separate fields of knowledge often a necessary prerequisite for solving the complex problems of our age. It is also true that radically new insights and developments often result from the friction between various domains of knowledge that arise in the boundary clash between well-established fields of knowledge. However, we know very little as yet about these 'boundary crossing' dynamics (see, however, Weick 1979 and 1995 for theoretical studies of 'sense-making' in such boundary crossing processes). We know that it is a prerequisite for dynamic interference that the knowledge systems that impact on each other are reciprocally closed. We also know that the one knowledge system observes the other on the basis of its own preconditions and it thus only able to come into contact with the other system on its own premises. Lastly, we know that it is in precisely such interference situations that the one knowledge system places its complexity at the disposal of the other system – in the form of something which the other system sees as an irritation. The precondition for this being able to happen is that a joint interaction and observation medium can be offered in which the one knowledge system can observe the other and vice versa, and thus reciprocally exploit the complexity that is at its disposal. A sure path to fiasco is for the one knowledge system to try to force the other system to adopt its own predominant control medium. To force the market or the hierarchy as a medium on the knowledge system is to undermine the innovation potential of the knowledge system.

Trust is sometimes named as such a boundary medium, although here I am sceptical. Instead, one could suggest investigating other boundary crossing possibilities. A popular example at present is to allow these boundary crossing zones to be based on contractual arrangements[9] Representatives of the two knowledge areas that meet and are to interfere enter into a contract regarding what services they are to supply under certain circumstances. The following three advantages of such a procedure are:

---

9   There are a few examples of such contract-based regulations in R&D agreements
    between private companies and research institutions but, as far as I know, no real
    studies have been undertaken of these contracts as boundary crossing media.

1. Robustness: Instead of a person-based relationship of trust, a formally regulated one is created. While the former is based on fulfilled expectations over time and therefore both takes time to establish and is susceptible to breaches of trust, one creates a relationship of trust that is based on explicit premises and possible sanctions.
2. Reciprocity: Entering into such a contract presupposes that each party places itself in the other's position and thereby aims at transcending the limitations of double contingency. In order to draw up a contract, the parties must reciprocally place themselves in the position of the other.
3. Inclusiveness: To interact within the framework of a contract means that reciprocal premises are established within which each of the players can operate on the basis of the functional logic of his own field of knowledge.

However, these forms of organisational and inter-organisational building-up of complexity have still not been systematically investigated. One could hypothetically assume that the richness of society depend, i.e. on the total amount of knowledge capital in its various forms, on the interaction between forms of knowledge capital and on their individual growth potential, e.g. in institutional frameworks of practice that differ from one form of knowledge capital to the next. Knowledge capital accumulates, partly by virtue of the interferences that characterise its circulation, from its systemic via its situative to its factual form of being.

Another – perhaps the most important and most predominant – boundary crossing medium is: Capital. 'Capital' is not, then, to be observed as a differentiation mechanism but as an effective, but therefore also brutal, structural coupling mechanism. It works because it refers to itself – what's in it for me, what isn't? – and on the basis of this it establishes couplings with the outside world: The business sells to the highest bidder, the company invests in what produces a profit, we do what pays off premises. In short, Capital makes things hold together, and it does so on its own premises. It does not presuppose any divine ruler or state authority that defines what is in and what is out, i.e. who is coupled and who is uncoupled.

If this is correct, it is not so strange that the so-called 'network economy' (which according to Castells is characterised by growth in complexity, partly because bureaucratic and other boundary-drawing is reduced and partly because the communicative range is radically increased) is accompanied by a growing spread (indeed, globalisation) of the capital relation. The explanation is that the capital relation is defined as a highly complex and effective structural form of coupling.

But, as we have also seen earlier, this connection between – in this case – an increase of complexity and an increase of structural coupling mechanisms is not a relation between problem and solution but one between a problem that is stabilised by the generation of an inner complexity that itself subsequently constitutes a problem, namely – in this case – that capital as a structural coupling produces a world market. The solution is therefore in itself a problem that is waiting for a solution.

Individual strategies for handling complexity: Self-practice as self-education

At the individual level as well one finds examples of the building-up of inner complexity. An analysis of this phenomenon is to be found in Lars Geer Hammershøj's dissertation *Selvdannelse og socialitet* [Self-education and sociality – the Danish word 'dannelse' corresponds to 'Bildung'] (Hammershøj 2003).

According to Lars Hammershøj, what he refers to as 'self-practice', i.e. to be educated or to educate oneself in modern society as opposed to earlier societies, has changed form in a radical sense. Via intensive use of Foucault's works he identifies three ideal-typical forms of 'Bildung':

The first ideal type is the 'Greco-Roman self-care'. Here, the focus is on self-mastery or self-control, so that life can be lived in accordance with Greek notions of the good life. The second ideal type is the 'Christian self-knowledge'. Here, focus is on gaining true insight into the depths of the self, so that it can be renounced or purified with the aim of attaining salvation. The third ideal type for the idea of education – the one that today represents the 'real' concept of 'Bildung' – is the 'neo-humanist', as formulated at the end of the 18th century. This concept of 'Bildung' comprises the following dimensions. Firstly, it presupposes the freedom of the individual to develop himself. But secondly, 'Bildung' has the nature of a transcendence of the self towards the greater – towards general humanity in its richest expression in cultural diversity, via the now identified national culture and the paradigmatic Greco-Antiquity culture. So in this conception there is a basic conflict between 'Bildung' and self-creation.

In our present time, however, one can in Hammershøj's opinion identify a new, fourth type of 'Bildung'. An early expression of this is to be found in Søren Kierkegaard's philosophical investigation of modern self, cf. the statement that the self is a relation that relates to itself. Today, this self-relating has become radicalised by it no longer being a question of creating an identity for oneself, i.e. an experience of being identical with oneself over time and at the same time different from others. No, the centre of the self-educating type of 'Bildung' is a taste-exercising self that is able to relate in such a way to his own taste-exercising. The aim of this self-education is to become a personality, i.e. to constitute an 'interesting taste-exercising'. The risk of course can be that one can want to wish not to be oneself and thereby become a taste-exercising with a distaste for oneself (cf. Hammershøj 2003: 138).

The mechanism is the same as the one I have previously emphasised – that an outer complexity pressure is met by an inner complexity build-up, i.e. an individual self-educating process. And the consequence can also be the same – that the answer to outer complexity itself becomes a complexity problem. For example, because such a taste-exercising with a distaste for oneself can express itself as a combination of extreme self-control and self-destruction. It may express itself in pathological fashion (cf. Hammershøj 2003: 312ff). It is also possible to claim, by the way, that this form of 'Bildung' is related to such other individual complexity handling strategies as 'readiness to adapt', etc.

The Internet's medial morphology

Until now, I have attempted to outline what I would call the social morphology of modern society in the form of a description and conceptualisation based on the theory of complexity, with examples of paradoxical forms of handling complexity at the levels of society, the organisation and the individual.

Another task in this connection is to characterise what one could call medial complexity handling – i.e. can one analyse dissemination media on the basis of the same complexity-paradigmatic approach? My own proposal (outlined in Qvortrup 2003) is to describe the medial morphology of the Internet on the basis of this approach.

It is a crucial point here that the Internet – as is also emphasised by Niels Ole Finnemann – contains a breadth of variation hitherto unknown. So one must be careful when associating it with particular social structures.

Nevertheless, I wish to advance the hypothesis that the Internet in the form of a hypertext system represents a building-up of inner complexity in the media and communications system that is apparently qualitatitively different from other centralistic media and communications systems (cf. Qvortrup 2003). This idea has been very much inspired by Peter Bøgh Andersen. His statement is that, based on the three vital components of the world wide web – a universal address system (the universal resource language, URL), a universal language (the hypertext transfer protocol, HTTP), and a system for self-reference, namely the hypertext markup language (HTML), a media system is created that builds up complexity by virtue of its own procedures and not because of an external entity, whether it be an editor or some other player. One text element refers to a second text element, which in turn refers to a third, etc. And not only that, a text element can also refer to a programme that can modify the programme that originally referred to it.

In other words, the assertion is that the Internet with the WWW system of addressing, protocols and self-referring links represents a medial complexity machine that at the same time constitutes a problem.

Hypercomplexity and social morphology

With the aid of these examples, I have outlined a 'social morphology' for the modern society that is based on the theory of complexity. My assertion is that it is conceptually more potent and usable than Castells' network concept, especially if one is interested in an epochal characterisation of modern society, i.e. is interested in modern society's *differentia specifica* and not where it resembles all other societies. It describes modern society, so to speak, from not only a different but, for certain purposes, a better point of observation. But this position too is naturally one in society and therefore equipped with its blind spot. What consequences that has, others are sure to be able to point out.

By means of this complexity paradigm an evolution paradigm of the type 'a problem that finds its solution' is not being indicated, but one that points to the fact that the problem is also the solution. Consequently, the solution represents a new potential problem. The basic principle is that only complexity reduces complexity. This implies that the problem of complexity is handled by complexity being inscribed in itself. The result is a provisional stability, which, however, will subsequently give rise to new instabilities.

This means that the concept 'network society' is not to be conceived as indicating a scientific point of observation but as an example of social self-descriptions. 'Network society' is a communicative trick, by means of which society can put an address on itself, whilst the paradoxicality of modern society – which is emphasised if one has an analysis of society with complexity as the 'Leitdifferenz' – is, from a semantic point of view, made indistinct.

Furthermore, I have indicated 'knowledge' as being a basic category in the complexity-theoretical analysis of society, because knowledge is a concept of certain expectations and therefore one of complexity handling. I have also indicated that even if complexity and knowledge come to take centre stage in the analysis of society, it is possible on the basis of a categorisation of forms of knowledge to identify the network categories that Castells advances in his analysis of society.

Lastly, I have briefly referred to functional differentiation, to the development of formal organisations and to individual self-educative strategies as other strategies for handling complexity; strategies which, like the knowledge strategy, answer outer complexity with inner complexity and therefore do not induce one to believe that the problem of complexity can be solved, but that it can be handled by being moved, so that it does not appear as a problem to do with outer complexity but as a problem related to inner complexity. The paradox can be summarised as follows: It is not so that the more we know, the less we do not know. Knowledge is not a zero-sum game. No: The more we know, the more we know that we do not know.

To avoid any misunderstanding, it ought, however, to be emphasised that the social morphology hereby outlined is not exclusive, and that there is no evolutionary necessity inherent in it. Other social morphologies can certainly co-exist and even oust differentiation-logical morphology. It is, for example, obvious in the present global-political situation that a very old centre-periphery differentiation is being re-introduced, based into the bargain on a just as old religious legitimisation. Indeed, instead of allowing legality and legitimacy to be concomitant, as Kant in an utopian fashion imagined at the end of the 18th century, currently the justification of legality would appear to be an ousted by a religious-imperialist justification of legitimacy.

As already mentioned, the consequence of this is a quite extremely comprehensive complexity-reducing gain. Once more, the world can be seen from an us/them perspective. But the consequence is also that the possibility for decentral self-regulation is reduced. This morphology, in other words, calls for a considerable power-political investment, which one may suspect will not help stability in the long run.

Similarly, it is important to stress that along with a growing functional differentiation there naturally also exists an almost infinite number of interaction systems that are loosely linked to each other. The point is, however, that these interaction systems with their reciprocally loose couplings cannot of themselves supply the complexity-handling potential made necessary by our present-day globalised societies in order to be possible as societies. For the same reason, the network concept is in itself insufficient, if one is interested in describing the *differentia specifica* of present-day society.

The most important point, however, is that the paradigm I am indicating here is not an evolutionary worse-better paradigm but one of paradox. It renounces the possibility of pointing to some outer cause for, and explanation of, the possibility of society and will always try to find this cause and explanation in society itself. It is therefore adequate to call this the paradigm of the hypercomplex.

A crucial characteristic of such a paradigm is that it deselects heteropoiesis (God, demon) in favour of autopoiesis. The adequate point of observation is not the one of God's or of the rational, order-creating demon's. The adequate point of observation is that of the joker.

That was why I mentioned above Carl Schmitt's concept of the sovereign. The sovereign is the heteropoietical means of de-paradoxicalising the paradox of society. My reply is that the sovereign is not a de-paradoxicalising formula but at the very most a contingency formula.

I therefore advanced above that social order is not created by the monarch with his regal power, the state with its power of the state or the people with its popular will moulding together the atoms of society to form a unity. No, social order is created by a diversity of communicative systems together creating an immensely complex and dynamic stability in the form of knowledge networks with special morphological characteristics. Society does not exist by virtue of the purity of the social order but by virtue of the complex impurity of the social structures.

We still do not know whether this actually represents the predominant present trend of developments in the global society. The question is whether a new sovereignty perhaps could offer global stabilisation with a subsequent updating of both the sovereign's stability understanding and his imperial centre-periphery differentiation morphology.

At this point, analysis must give way to a poorly justified hope – the hope that today in a globalised society of hitherto unseen complexity we dare believe that the sovereign cannot stabilise himself as a God, indeed, not ever as a political-military demon, but that he can only function in the guise of a joker – as the ever-topical card that society itself can play in the continuing game of itself.

References

Bak, P. (1996). *How Nature Works. The Science of Self-Organized Criticality.* New York: Springer Verlag.

Baecker, D. (2000). Die Theorieform des Systems. In *Soziale Systeme. Zeitschrift für soziologische Theorie.* Jg. 6, no. 2: 213-236.

Bateson, G. (2000). The Logical Categories of Learning and Communication. In G. Bateson, *Steps to an Ecology of Mind.* Chicago and London: The University of Chicago Press.

Bell, D. (1973). *The Coming of Post-Industrial Society.* New York: Basic Books.

Spencer Brown, G. (1971). *Laws of Form.* London: George Allen and Unwin.

Castells, M. (1996). *The Rise of the Network Society.* Malden, MA and Oxford, UK: Blackwell Publishers.

Castells, M. (1997). *The Power of Identity.* Malden, MA and Oxford, UK: Blackwell Publishers.

Castells, M. (1998). *End of Millennium.* Malden, MA and Oxford, UK: Blackwell Publishers.

Castells, M. (2000). Materials for an exploratory theory of the network society. In *British Journal of Sociology*, 51/1.

Dertouzos, M.L. (1997). *What Will Be: How the New World of Information Will Change Our Lives.* San Francisco: HarperEdge.

Distinktion (2001). *Tidsskrift for samfundsteori*. No. 2, Special issue on Carl Schmitt and the question of sovereignty.

Drucker, P.F. (1969). *The Age of Discontinuity: Guidelines to Our Changing Society.* London: Heinemann.

Finnemann, N. O. (2005). *Internettet i mediehistorisk perspektiv.* Copenhagen: Forlaget Samfundslitteratur.

Hammershøj, L.G. (2003). *Selvdannelse og socialitet.* Copenhagen: Danmarks Pædagogiske Universitetsforlag.

Jones, S.G. (1998). *Cybersociety 2.0.* Thousand Oaks et al.: Sage Publications.

Latour, B. (1999). *Pandora's Hope. Essays on the Reality of Science Studies.* Cambridge, MA and London, England: Harvard University Press.

Luhmann, N. (1990). Ich sehe was, was du nicht siehst. In *Soziologische Aufklärung 5, Konstruktivistische Perspektiven.* Opladen: Westdeutscher Verlag: 228-234.

Luhmann, N. (1990a). *Die Wissenschaft der Gesellschaft.* Frankfurt a.M.: Suhrkamp Verlag.

Luhmann, N. (1995) [German original:1984]. *Social Systems.* Stanford CA: Stanford University Press.

Luhmann, N. (1997). *Die Gesellschaft der Gesellschaft.* Frankfurt a.M.: Suhrkamp Verlag.

Luhmann, N. (2000). '"Hvad er tilfældet?" og "Hvad ligger bag?" De to sociologier og samfundsteorien' ['"What is the Case?" and "What Lies Behind It?" The Two Sociologies and the Theory of Society']. In *Distinktion. Tidsskrift for samfundsteori.* No. 1: 9-26.

Luhmann, N. (2002). *Das Erziehungssystem der Gesellschaft.* Frankfurt a.M.: Suhrkamp Verlag.

Luhmann, N. and Schorr, K.E. (1988). *Reflexionsprobleme im Erziehungssystem.* Frankfurt a.M.: Suhrkamp Verlag.

Negroponte, N. (1995). *Being Digital.* New York: Alfred A. Knopf.

OECD (2004). *Innovations in the Knowledge Economy.* Paris: OECD.

Penrose, E. (1959). *The Theory of the Growth of the Firm.* Oxford: Oxford University Press.

Qvortrup, L. (1998). *Det hyperkomplekse samfund* [The hypercomplex society]. Copenhagen: Gyldendal.

Qvortrup, L. (2001). *Det lærende samfund* [The learning society]. Copenhagen: Gyldendal.

Qvortrup, L. (2003). *The Hypercomplex Society*. New York: Peter Lang.

Qvortrup, L. (2004). *Det vidende samfund* [The knowing society]. Copenhagen: Unge pædagoger.

Schmitt, C. (2001) [1922]. Politisk teologi. Suverænitetens definition. In *Distinktion. Tidsskrift for samfundsteori*, No. 2.

Schmitt, C. (2002) [1932]. *Det politiskes begreb*. Copenhagen: Hans Reitzels Forlag.

Serres, M. (1980). *Le parasite*. Paris: Editions Grasset et Fasquelle.

Serres, M. (1997). *The Troubadour of Knowledge*. Ann Arbor: The University of Michigan Press [translated from Le Tiers-Instruit. François Bourin, Paris 1991].

Simmel, G. (1998) [1908]. Sociologiens problem. In *Hvordan er samfund muligt? Udvalgte sociologiske skrifter*. Copenhagen: Gyldendal.

Weick, K.E. (1979). *The Social Psychology of Organizing*. 2nd Edition. New York: Random House.

Weick, K.E. (1995). *Sensemaking in Organizations*. Thousand Oaks CA: Sage.

Wenger, E., McDermott, R. and Snyder, W.M (2002). *Cultivating Communities of Practice*. Boston MA: Harvard Business School Press.

Network Society

I. Complexity

Take self-organization as a paradigm to conceive the nature of society. Self-organization is an observer's answer to the question of how a phenomenon is able to reproduce, given that traditional scientific explanations, such as causality and statistics, fail, because that phenomenon consists of neither few and heterogeneous variables (suitable for causal explanations), nor of many and homogeneous variables (suitable for statistic explanations). Warren Weaver called such a phenomenon a complex one (Weaver 1948). It challenges an observer to acknowledge that it knows more of itself than the observer is able to comprehend. The observer is thus called upon to forego any attempt to "understand" the phenomenon, and instead to "control" his interaction with that phenomenon in such a way that he is able to relate what he might be doing or refraining from doing with what happens – never being sure, of course, whether what he is observing "is" the phenomenon as such or rather his interaction with it (Ashby 1958; Morin 1974; Glanville 1987).

Society is such a phenomenon to be called complex, since it consists of large numbers of heterogeneous variables which defy any causal or statistic description and explanation. Society should even be called "hypercomplex", since it not only is, for an observer, complex, but also describes itself as such, thus adding the knowledge of being beyond traditional ways of scientific explanation to its own complexity (Fuchs 1992; Luhmann 1997; Qvortrup 2003).

The paradigm of self-organization is a paradoxical one. In drawing a distinction between the observer and a phenomenon, it consists in understanding the observer's world as the necessary context of the phenomenon's reproduction. Thus, the self-organization of society does not just happen out there, but calls upon the observer to be concomitantly performed by him. Any notion of the nature of society, therefore, has to take into account the performing observer's contribution to the reproduction of society. By "nature", we mean once again a paradoxical process of reproduction, which combines constant decay (or entropy) with ever-renewing form (neg-entropy) (Luhmann 1995a). At any one instant in the reproduction of society, an observer is called upon to relate the form just dissolving to a form just emerging. Quantum physics comes to mind, which has a fundamental indeterminacy solved, i.e. temporarily translated into, or confused with, determination, by an observer deciding on his choices. Louis H. Kauffman calls "network synthesis" such an introduction of markers which transform indeterminate into determinate expressions (Kauffman 1978).

As abstract as these considerations relating to a possible paradigm to conceive the nature of society may seem, they should not come as a surprise to a reader acquainted with sociological theory. Ever since sociology began to consider society, it has offered notions of society which conform to an operational understanding of a society, even though the inclusion of the observer has only recently been acknowledged. Auguste Comte explicitly speaks of the disorganization and reorganization of a society going from its theological and metaphysical to its scientific state, requiring its observers to forego any empty, because anarchical, criticism in favor of a political understanding of the necessities of production (Comte 2000). Karl Marx and Friedrich Engels think rather similarly of capitalism as the vaporization of anything resembling a corporative society and require its observers to engage in a revolution, transforming society into one which finally has a no-nonsense view of human life and relations (Marx/Engels 1998). Classical sociology continues that line of thought, albeit by doing away with any notion of progress (and redemption) or decadence (and damnation). Gabriel Tarde conceives society as a state of association, reproducing via a strict discontinuity of its elements, yet homogeneity of the being of these elements (Tarde 1999). Emile Durkheim looks at the abstract complementarity (and, thus, necessary even if difficult solidarity) of the corporations and professions to be distinguished and separated by their taking part in the social division of labour, when considering the organization of society (Durkheim 1998). Georg Simmel thinks of society as a sum of forms of relations constantly engaging individuals and their historical reality within processes of synthesis that emerge and dissolve (Simmel 1950). Max Weber focuses on either subjectively felt community ("*Vergemeinschaftung*") or on the rational choice of relations ("*Vergesellschaftung*"), the latter being by definition a process of constant re-negotiation (Weber 1978). And Talcott Parsons goes all the way back to Aristotle's *Politics* to denote by society that social system which self-sufficiently is able to produce and reproduce the fulfilment of all functions necessary to produce and reproduce itself (Parsons 1966).

The nature of society thus has been regarded as an "autopoietical" process long before that notion has been introduced with respect to "living systems" by Humberto R. Maturana and Francisco J. Varela (Maturana/Varela 1980). Society must certainly not be considered a living system, yet it features its own kind of "cognitive" self-organization, if "cognitive" refers to an ability to distinguish between what is useful for reproduction, and what is not. Nothing, of course, guarantees that such a distinction, as made by a self-organizing society, is in accordance with an understanding of usefulness held by the human observers engaged by that society.

Following Niklas Luhmann, we propose to look at processes of "communication" when watching how a complex and therefore self-organizing society engages its observers in reproducing itself (Luhmann 1995b and 1997). Communication here means that any one observer when trying to determine the indeterminate, produces

97

degrees of freedom of choices which call for their own conditioning, i.e., framing, to become options of real action. This is like in Claude E. *Shannon's Mathematical Theory of Communication:* You have to accept a set of (other) possibilities if you are going to produce, i.e., to select, any one of them (Shannon/Weaver 1963); you may even consider actually producing that wealth of unknown other possibilities by selectively doing what you are doing (Luhmann 1995). This is the single idea we need to address in the paradoxes mentioned above: Society reproduces as an indeterminate set of possibilities the very moment any one possibility is taken up by one or several of its observers. In the mathematical theory of communication undertaken in engineering, that set of possibilities is a determinate one, thus going for a probabilistic calculus of information and communication. In sociology, we propose to drop that assumption of a determinate set of possibilities in favor of an indeterminate one, turning the set of possibilities into a context, contextualized by the very operation of being chosen (Gumperz 1982; Auer/di Luzio 1992), thus going for a possibilistic calculus of information and communication (Baecker 2005). We draw on the mathematics of George Spencer-Brown to consider such a possibilistic calculus consisting in distinctions being called and crossed, and defining forms which comprise the two sides of a distinction, the operation of the distinction, and the space brought about by the distinction being drawn (Spencer-Brown 1994).

II. Coding

Let us start our description of network society by recalling the simple, yet powerful mechanism of producing and dealing with social uncertainty proposed and developed by Harrison C. White in his eponymous *Identity and Control* (White 1992). Networks are considered to consist of, and reproduce, a number of heterogeneous elements, such as ideologies, institutions, individuals, technologies, and sites, tied to one another via relations of identity and control. There is no one element not receiving its identity from the relations it is tied into. And there is no way to maintain identity if not via the control of the contribution of one's own identity to all other identities. That includes expressions of identities which consist in imposing themselves on others, and depend for that imposition on the others accepting that it is one way or another. Thus, identity, as well as control, is mutual, or cybernetic (Glanville 1987).

All we need to be able to understand, i.e. control, as regards the self-organization of a society is to look at networks being constituted by elements of any, yet necessarily heterogeneous, kind tying themselves into relations of mutual identity and control (Latour 1996). The heterogeneity is necessary as a reminder of indeterminacy and uncertainty, and thus of the complexity calling any one observer to make up his or her mind for him- or herself. The heterogeneity is finally necessary as a reminder of the impossibility of being sure what identity one is dealing with (including one's own) from any one moment to the next, as unknown processes of dissolution and re-emergence may be happening in between.

A network society is in principle an ecological one, in that it comes without any super-system encompassing all networks and giving them some order rendered by any external reference. Instead, a network society excels in neighborhood relationships which exhibit all kinds of consensus and conflict functional for the self-maintenance of the networks involved. That is, even networks among themselves only add to networks, thus giving society its unavoidable structure of self-similarity (Turner 1997; Fuchs 2001; Abbott 2001).

If networks define the structure of a network society, we may call the distinction between identity and control the code of that society, given that a code may be understood as a distinction able to translate unspecified events into internal events that produce some kind of information (Ruesch/Bateson 1987). Any code must combine resonance with connectivity, or variety with redundancy, to be able at any instant to produce that kind of information which contextualizes any one message by the set of possibilities it is selected from. Identity and control seem to be able to ensure just that as identity is open to self-determination and self-indeterminacy, and control means attempt and success as well as ignorance and failure.

Relying on Spencer-Brown's notation of form, we may thus define the network as follows:

$$\text{network} \quad = \quad \overline{\text{control}\,|\,}\text{identity}$$

We give "control" the status of the operation drawing the distinction of the network, that operation calling up the context of "identity", like a commitment one is expected to bring with one and exhibit if any attempt to control is to succeed, thus adding constraint, i.e., determination (calling up new sources of indeterminacy), to possibility (Elster 2000). This means that networks are constituted by attempts to control by attributing identities to all elements involved.

Spencer-Brown's notion of "form" (Spencer-Brown 1997; Baecker 1999) enables us to look at three features of such a distinction. The first feature is that all distinctions only come about by being operated by first-order observers being watched by second-order observers. Distinctions are not categories to order the world, but operations produced by observers, and watched by other observers. They produce a reality brought about via second-order observations, so that this reality by one and the same token is both indeterminate and self-determining (Luhmann 1992). The second feature is that any one distinction, by being drawn, constitutes its own form, consisting of its two sides and the separating line of distinction viewed together within the space that distinction opens up when and by being drawn. This means that any one distinction, when looked at with respect to its form, defines the connection and correlation of two terms being distinguished without having to specify how this connection and correlation come about if not precisely by the distinction distinguishing the two terms. The notion of the form of a distinction thus looks at the space of operations severed and explored by that operation of distinction. And the third feature is the "re-entry" of the operation of the distinction into the space of the distinction such that for instance "identity", on one hand, gets its focus by being distinguished from "control", and vice versa, in such a way that, on the other hand, "identity" and "control" become indistinguishable by being connected to each other, calling for the same distinction to be drawn again if the form of the network is to reproduced. This may remind the reader of the philosophical and literary endeavor of "deconstruction", which was able to show that we, observers of our society, only trust distinctions we are able to distrust as well. The indeterminate yet determinable reality constituted by second-order observers is a reality perfecting itself out of its own corruption, and corrupting itself due to its own perfection. That is why ambivalence is the first and last word to be spoken with respect to both the kind of reality our society is embedded in and producing, and our stance towards that reality.

III. Meaning

The network society is a world society. Its meaning horizon is the world as a whole, which means that any one actualization of meaning is to be compared with, and severed from, all other actualizations of meaning which come to the mind of any one of the identities involved. To handle the enormous overflow of meaning present at any one moment, the network society relies on cultural forms which allow it to deal highly selectively with the meaning it has access to. Niklas Luhmann proposes distinguishing three cultural forms with respect to dominant communication media, as there are: manuscripts in Antiquity, print in modern times, and the computer, including the Internet, in our next society: He outlines Aristotelian *telos* for the writing culture, Cartesian self-reference for modern culture, and perhaps a Spencer-Brownian form for our culture as three selective devices which allow one to go for dynamic stability in the midst of the instability unleashed by a wealth of new meaning accessible (Luhmann 1997; Baecker 2006).

If we concentrate here on our society, the next society (Drucker 2001), we can outline the cultural form as the selective device able to handle the surplus meaning of the computer and the Internet culture, which sometimes is taken to be the culture of a network society coming of age (Castells 1996). The cultural form of the Spencer-Brownian calculus means that any one meaning is dealt with according to a pattern relating possible next operations included and an unknown horizon of other possibilities excluded. That is, as in operational research proposed by W. Ross Ashby (Ashby 1958), the one and only question to be dealt with and to be decided at any one instant is what possibly to do (or forego) next while knowing that there is a context, or frame, one is ignorant of and possibly has to turn one's attention to the very next moment.

If the general notion of form in Spencer-Brown reads as follows:

$$\text{form} \quad = \quad \overline{\text{marked state}} \mid \text{unmarked state}$$

and if the unmarked state stands for the indeterminate as the excluded other side of the distinction included into the form, we can specify that general notion for the particular case of meaning by saying:

$$\text{meaning} \quad = \quad \overline{\text{actual}} \mid \text{possible}$$

Note that this is an understanding of meaning which is compatible with philosophy, sociology, and economics (Whitehead 1979; Luhmann 1995; Shackle 1972).

For all specifics of meaning we may adhere to the three dimensions of meaning distinguished by Niklas Luhmann, which are the factual, the social, and the temporal (Luhmann 1995). Any communication, i.e., any action and experience, in network society would thus take the form of a non-linear sequence of choices distinguishing actual insides of affairs, actual performances within certain milieux, and actual present time horizons, from possible outsides, possible audiences, and possible futures:

$$\text{affair} \quad = \quad \overline{\text{inside}} \mid \text{outside}$$

$$\text{milieu} \quad = \quad \overline{\text{performance}} \mid \text{audience}$$

```
time horizon = present | future
```

This is to say that all communication and action drawing on meaning and producing meaning in a network society relies on a combination of subject mater, milieu, and time horizon to take its actual choices within the context of possible other choices. All affairs are affairs consisting of a certain inside of a matter, to be compared, at any instant, with possible outsides of more or less relevance. Any milieu is a milieu produced by performances searching for, and finding, their audience, framed by a general experience of publics as switching devices between networks (Goffman 1959; White 1995). And any time horizon has to be chosen with respect to unknown futures with more or less relevance to the present, selected and identified with or without reference to a certain past.

Note that there is a certain affinity between the temporal dimension of meaning and its overall form in that the future is by definition unmarked. That may be the reason why the next society is best coordinated with respect to its unknown future as institutionalized in uncertain investment projects in the market economy, uncertain chances of re-election in democratic politics, uncertain fates of love in passionate relations of intimacy, the interest of art in newness, or in the never-ending process of theoretical curiosity in the sciences. This kind of coordination with respect to the unknown future organizes more complexity than any social ordering of the society or factual ordering of the matters to be dealt with could possibly do. That is why the complexity of the next society is a temporal one (Luhmann 1997), and why all meaning has no other choice but to look for its respective present anchors, framed by an unknown future, marked as the unmarked state.

What is more, we may witness another change of the temporal order of society by relying more and more on a distinction between event and process, which displaces the older distinctions between fleetingness (or vanity) and eternity, for pre-modern society, and between past, present, and future, for modern society. Event and process relate the moment and its possible, yet uncertain and risky, and promising or dangerous, context, frame, and development in such a way that any one moment cannot gain its dynamic stability unless by looking at just the very next moment it may able to link to, or to refer back to. There is of course no eternity any more in distinction to all that fleetingness which would guarantee some kind of self-identical recursion, anchored in some transcendental infinity. Instead, we are always dealing in finite singularities, which constitute a world that is the ecological unity of the difference between one singularity and possible other singularities (Heidegger 1995). And there is no historical identity of past, present, and future any more, to be distinguished with respect to epochs, and to be taken seriously with respect to memory, duty, and expectation. Instead, we are invited to surround any one event we may wish to rely on with its own horizon of past, present, and future, only to be constructed with respect to almost instant deconstruction. Time becomes a gift, which we give and receive, making up our sometimes local, sometimes global accounts of whom to include into, and exclude from, it, what to focus on, and what not, and how long to insist on it for what reasons (Derrida 1991).

IV. Structure and Evolution

There is more structure to this kind of network society than just networks. We may notice, following again Niklas Luhmann, that there are interactions, organizations, social movements, and some society of its own, which are remarkably self-similar and exhibit patterns of communication and action nobody really has difficulties in identifying, in distinguishing, and in getting along with (Luhmann 1997; Baecker 2005).

Interactions consist of communication among people present. By exhibiting their own form, which consists in the inclusion of the absents excluded, they deal with the question how to get along with those present given that others, specified and unspecified, are absent

(Goffman 1959). Organizations extend the reach of possible communication and action, including "collective" action, to people not necessarily present by restricting the possible reach to members only of any one organization and by having to translate "diffuse" communication into "specific" decisions which add a form of the regulation of decisions to the open form of the iteration of communication (Simon 1997). Social movements are restricted neither to those present nor to members. Instead they can only use the medium of "protest". This implies that they relate to issues that cause disturbance or fury that are, in turn, attributed to certain people or institutions responsible for these issues. One tends to believe that all this can be avoided if only things were better organized or if one could exclude certain people from certain business areas. Social movements reproduce as long as the protest works, and vanish as soon as cause and emotion, address and countermeasures lose their evidence. The only pattern or even "system" which is able to reproduce with unspecified, still undetermined meanings of communication is society itself. It consists of all communication possible, viewed from any one instantiation of it. It is a measure of possible reach, describing the global as "small" and the local as "rich" (Watts 1999; Leifer 1991).

All of these structures are to be considered as Spencer-Brownian forms, so that social self-organization at any moment takes place with respect to both the respective selections chosen (people present, members, protest cause, communication) and the unmarked state as the substitute symbol for the indeterminate, yet determinable other side of the distinction (people absent, non-members, loss of protest cause, silence). We thus can proceed with our description of the network society by saying that it consists of a non-linear and heterarchic network among the following structures, each of them, except for the society, coming in plenty, if not a mass of instantiations. The society, given that it is the world society, comes only in one copy, strange as that may appear (Stichweh 2000). We have the following forms, and it seems they sum up neatly what self-similar structures network society provides us with:

interaction   =   presence | absence

organization   =   members | non-members

social movement   =   protest | affirmation

society   =   communication

Extensive empirical research might possibly ensue, looking, among many other issues, into the structuring of interaction via absent gods, friends, foes, and relatives; of organization via the seeking of balance towards non-member clients, investors, stake-holders, and regulators; of social movements via the unavoidability of participating in the same society the protest is addressed to; or of society seeking to recruit individuals, people, given that these rely on their senses, their reasons, and their idiosyncrasies when judging whether and how to partake in any kind of communication.

This kind of research may realize that and how social institutions are already tuned to manage the form of distinctions connecting their terms by separating them, such as religion, viewed as an endeavour in the regulation of behaviour with respect to both interaction and motivation (Weber 1988), or capital markets enforcing the interests of non-members on the members of an enterprise (Jensen 1993), or trade unions searching for reasons to accept the same jobs whose terms of trade they tend to refuse (Baecker 2004), or art presenting society with the communication of excluded perceptions of colour, sound, taste, and meaning, only to experience that it gets tamed and framed with reference to the beautiful, to the sublime, or just to culture (Adorno 1997).

Add to the knowledge of structure a knowledge of evolution and you end up with a first and simple, yet already rather rich picture of the network society self-organizing. It is simple with respect to received sociological wisdom, yet rich with respect to a possible algorithm of communication, or a Whitean "calculus of trade-offs in uncertainty" (White 1992: 17), which describes the sensitivity and robustness, the switches and recursions any one communication at any one moment exhibits.

Evolution comes in three mechanisms: variation, selection, and retention (Campbell 1969; Luhmann 1997). They tell you once again that any event is part of a network, be it a network searched after, one to be avoided, or one intervening as a surprise to those involved. Any one event may turn out to be a variation to be selected negatively or positively if it does not just disappear the moment it appears. Any one event may also turn out to select other events to either go with it or not. Any one event may even turn out to put into perspective a whole range of other events so that they become accommodated to some pre-selected frame which acts as a kind of bottleneck to the event selected. In social evolution at least, there is no telling which events belong to what kind of mechanism, since any one of them may become recruited by different networks with respect to all three mechanisms.

Take sociological theory as an example. What is a sociological theory in terms of evolution? It is a variation mechanism with respect to other theories. It says No to them and pursues some different track. It is also a selection mechanism, which may be responsible for a whole range of facts never to be seen again and a different range of facts to be looked at for the first time in their life. The theory may even define new kinds of facts, like those which defy received methods of empirical research because they deal with unmarked states, being ways of communication to handle its own ignorance and uncertainty (Luhmann 1997: chap. 1. II). And it may be a retention mechanism showing how both theory and facts are to be regarded within the sociological tradition so that it can become a part of it without risking destroying it. It makes sense to distinguish a scientific event like the emergence of a theory with respect to all three mechanisms of evolution, even when all three play their role in such a way that the theory does not neatly fall into the range of any one of them. It makes sense because the reasons to invest work into that theory, or the reasons to refuse and even fight it, might be rather different reasons when it comes to investing in, or fighting, variation, selection, or retention. Variation may be well received since it broadens the evolutionary pool of the whole discipline. Selection may be looked at more sceptically since it threatens, or seduces, to ally with facts and methods in such a way that it becomes stronger and stronger. Retention, then, may attract both followers and opponents, since the perspective is to serve the discipline which is welcomed by everybody anyway. Kuhn's paradigms, thus, are textbook examples of products and premises of self-organization with respect to both their inertia and their agitation (Kuhn 1962).

Evolutionary mechanisms, as applied to social form, act like a guarantee and master clock for all events constituting elements of a network. They provide for the essential self-diversity that is part of any self-identity (Whitehead 1979: 25). Looking at an element in terms of the event it is, it falls apart into being different events to different observer perspectives embedded within different networks.

V. Knots

Let us conclude our enquiry of self-organizing complexity, networks, recursive forms (or even *eigen*-forms), and evolution (Kauffman 1987; Kauffman/Varela 1980; Varela 1979). What you end up with are knots of communication and action, which bring together indeterminacy, determination, and self-reference. Any one of these knots, a milieu of certain people, an organization searching for its purpose, a society giving a bonus to conventions obeyed, or a social movement insisting on the morality of its protest, is a network about to dissolve and to re-establish itself from the indeterminate set of possibilities it has just added to.

If it were not for the markers adding their prejudices and insisting on their choices (Kauffman 1978), that kind of network society would be far too improbable to stand any evolutionary chance. As far as we know, these markers are human beings, fragile, finite, and solitary. Yet it is they who know how to tell events and processes apart. And it is they who with any event look for a different one, trying to check on their opportunity costs, and who in any process come up with just enough inconsistency, groundlessness, and imagination to keep things and networks alive (Heidegger 1995: §49).

These human beings have nothing to invest but their observations, including second-order observations of observers coming as their own knots of networks, focusing on them or just keeping their distance from them. That is the operation providing networks with the information they need, if in-formation is just another word for a knot coming undone or being cut.

References

Abbott, A. (2001). *Chaos of Disciplines*. Chicago: Chicago University Press.

Adorno, T.W. (1997). *Aesthetic Theory*. Transl. and ed. R. Hullot-Kentor. London: Athlone Press.

Ashby, W.R. (1958). Requisite Variety and Its Implications for the Control of Complex Systems. In *Cybernetica*, 1: 83-99.

Auer, P. and di Luzio, A. (eds.) (1992). *The Contextualization of Language*. Amsterdam: Benjamins.

Baecker, D. (ed.) (1999). *Problems of Form*. Transl. M. Irmscher with L. Edwards. Stanford: Stanford University Press.

Baecker, D. (2004). Wozu Gewerkschaften? In *Mittelweg 36: Zeitschrift des Hamburger Instituts für Sozialforschung* 13, June/July: 3-20.

Baecker, D. (2005). *Form und Formen der Kommunikation*. Frankfurt a.M.: Suhrkamp.

Baecker, D. (2006). Niklas Luhmann in the Society of the Computer. In *Cybernetics and Human Knowing* 13.

Campbell, D.T. (1969). Variation and Selective Retention in Socio-Cultural Evolution. In *General Systems*, 14: 69-85.

Castells, M. (1996). *The Rise of the Network Society*. Oxford: Blackwell.

Comte, A. (2000). *Système de politique positive*. Paris: Vrin.

Derrida, J. (1991). *Donner le temps: 1. La fausse monnaie*. Paris: Galilée.

Drucker, P.F. (2001). The next society. In *The Economist*, November 3rd.

Durkheim, E. (1998). *De la division du travail social*. Paris: PUF.

Elster, J. (2000). *Ulysses Unbound: Studies in Rationality, Precommitment, and Constraints*. Cambridge: Cambridge University Press.

Fuchs, P. (1992). *Die Erreichbarkeit der Gesellschaft: Zur Konstitution und Imagination gesellschaftlicher Einheit*. Frankfurt a.M.: Suhrkamp.

Fuchs, S. (2001). Networks. In *Soziale Systeme: Zeitschrift für soziologische Theorie*, 7: 125-155.

Glanville, R. (1987). The Question of Cybernetics. In *Cybernetics and Systems*, 18: 99-112.

Goffman, E. (1959). *The Presentation of Self in Everyday Life*. New York: Anchor Books.

Gumperz, J. (1982). *Discourse Strategies*. Cambridge: Cambridge University Press.

Heidegger, M. (1995). *The Fundamental Concepts of Metaphysics: World, Finitude, Solitude* (GA29/30). Transl. W. McNeill and N. Walker Bloomington, Ind: Indiana University Press.

Jensen, M.C. (1993). The Modern Industrial Revolution, Exit, and the Failure of Internal Control Systems. In *Journal of Finance*, 48: 831-880.

Kauffman, L.H. (1978). Network Synthesis and Varela's Calculus. In *International Journal of General Systems*, 4: 179-187.

Kauffman, L.H. (1987). Self-Reference and Recursive Forms. In *Journal of Social and Biological Structure* 10: 53-72.

Kauffman, L.H. and Varela, F.J. (1980). Form Dynamics. In *Journal of Social and Biological Structure*, 3: 171-206.

Kuhn, T.S. (1962). *The Structure of Scientific Revolutions*. Chicago: Chicago University Press.

Latour, B. (1996). On Actor-Network Theory: A Few Clarifications. In *Soziale Welt*, 47: 369-381.

Leifer, E.M. (1991). *Actors as Observers: A Theory of Skill in Social Relationships*. New York: Garland.

Luhmann, N. (1992). *Beobachtungen der Moderne*. Opladen: Westdeutscher Verlag.

Luhmann, N. (1995a). Über Natur. In: ders., *Gesellschaftsstruktur und Semantik: Studien zur Wissenssoziologie der modernen Gesellschaft*, Bd 4. Frankfurt a. M.: Suhrkamp: 9-30.

Luhmann, N. (1995b). *Social Systems*. Transl. by J. Bednarz, Jr. with D. Baecker. Stanford: Stanford University Press.

Luhmann, N. (1997). *Die Gesellschaft der Gesellschaft*. Frankfurt a. M.: Suhrkamp.

Marx, K. and Engels, F. (1998). *The Communist Manifesto*. New York: Oxford University Press.

Maturana, H.R. and Varela, F.J. (1980). *Autopoiesis and Cognition: The Realization of the Living*. Dordrecht: Reidel.

Morin, E. (1974). Complexity. In *International Social Science Journal*, 26: 555-582.

Parsons, T. (1966). *Societies: Evolutionary and Comparative Perspectives*. Englewood Cliffs, NJ: Prentice-Hall.

Qvortrup, L. (2003). *The Hypercomplex Society*. New York: Peter Lang.

Ruesch, J. and Bateson, G. (1987). *Communication: The Social Matrix of Psychiatry*. New York: Norton.

Shackle, G.L.S. (1972). *Epistemics and Economics: A Critique of Economic Doctrine*. Cambridge: Cambridge University Press.

Shannon, C.E. and Weaver, W. (1963). *The Mathematical Theory of Communication*. Urbana, Ill: Illinois University Press.

Simmel, G. (1950). *The Sociology of Georg Simmel*. Transl., ed. and with an introd. by K.H. Wolff. Glencoe, Ill: Free Press.

Simon, H.A. (1997). *Administrative Behavior: A Study of Decision-Making Processes in Administrative Organization*. 4th ed., New York: Free Pr.

Spencer-Brown, G. (1994). *Laws of Form*. Limited Edition. Portland, Ore: Cognizer Pr.

Stichweh, R. (2000). *Die Weltgesellschaft: Soziologische Analysen*. Frankfurt a.M.: Suhrkamp.

Tarde, G. (1999). *Monadologie et sociologie*. Le Plessis-Robinson: Institut Synthélabo.

Turner, F. (1997). Chaos and Social Science. In R.A. Eve, S. Horsfall and M.E. Lee (eds.). *Chaos, Complexity, and Sociology: Myths, Models, and Theories*. Thousand Oaks, Cal: Sage, xi-xxvii.

Varela, F.J. (1979). *Principles of Biological Autonomy*. New York: North Holland.

Watts, D. (1999). *Small Worlds: The Dynamics of Networks Between Order and Randomness*. Princeton: Princeton University Press.

Weaver, W. (1948). Science and Complexity. In *American Scientist*, 36: 536-544.

Weber, M. (1978). *Economy and Society: An Outline of Interpretive Sociology*. G. Roth and C. Wittich (eds.), transl. E. Fischoff et al. Berkeley: University of California Press.

Weber, M. (1988). *Gesammelte Aufsätze zur Religionssoziologie*. 3 vols. Marianne Weber (ed.). Tübingen: Mohr.

White, H.C. (1992). *Identity and Control: A Structural Theory of Action*. Princeton, NJ: Princeton University Press.

White, H.C. (1995). Network Switchings and Bayesian Forks: Reconstructing the Social and Behavioral Sciences. In *Social Research*, 62: 1035-1063.

Whitehead, A.N. (1979). *Process and Reality: An Essay in Cosmology*. Corrected Edition, D.R. Griffin and D.W. Sherburne (eds.). New York: Free Pr.

The Work of Art as a Network – Towards a Post-Deconstructive Aesthetics

It is with some hesitation that I offer a contribution to the discussion about the network society. I am afraid my approach to the matter may appear a little out of key. My angle is not at all sociological and I am not going to discuss aesthetics in the era of the network. If I have followed the debates about globalisation and world art correctly, adequate questions in this area seem to be of the following kind: Does the world market enhance or decrease the autonomy of art? Does the omnipresence of the Internet force all local forms of art into a homogenized and global set of forms, genres and styles – or does it rather allow for the development of new blends of heterogeneous and multicultural forms of art? Interesting as these questions may be, I do not feel particularly equipped to answer them. My hunch is that the answers should probably be found in a dialectics of both/and, but, for lack of experience and qualifications in this area, I shall leave it to sociologists of art to pursue the discussion.

By contrast, my approach is that of an aesthetician. I shall, in fact, be asking an age-old question once again: How may we conceive the work of art? If I hope to say something of relevance in this context, after all, it is due to the fact that – as a tentative answer to the question – I would like to suggest that we may begin looking at the work of art in terms of a network. Furthermore, I shall develop this idea by way of a theoretical platform based on a philosophy of difference which, I hope, will prove fitting for the post-ontological framework of mind which underlies this book.

My contribution will take the form of a presentation of the theoretical itinerary that has taken me to suggest that we may conceive the work of art as a network. I should probably warn the reader that this approach is not free of charge. Because I need to prepare the grounds for my suggestion, it will take me quite a while before I get to the point at which I can explain what, in my opinion, it might imply to start seeing the work of art in terms of a network. For the sake of increasing the suspense a little, I would like to advertise that the aim of my reflections is to introduce an aesthetics which may be construed as *post-deconstructive*.

The criticism of the self-contained work of art

I imagine that it will come as no surprise for anybody if I claim that, in the twentieth century, the classical notion of a self-contained and coherent work of art has been heavily criticised. In particular, the criticism has focused on two aspects: the *temporality* of the work of art and the active participation of the *recipient* in the formation of the work of art. To focus on these two dimensions means doubting that the meaning of a work of art may be guaranteed by the coherent structure of the work itself – that the limit of a valid interpretation is to be found at the physical borderlines of the work of art, so to speak. Insisting on the temporality implies that the semantics of a work of art ought not to be 'spatialised' as if it may be reduced to a particular meaning at a certain point in time. Similarly, insisting that it takes a recipient to fulfil a work of art comes down to saying that the work of art does, in fact, have no definite limits. A criticism based on these two assumptions may be found in many current theoretical positions. Let me just mention three evident examples.

1) The aesthetics of reception, known from, for instance, Umberto Eco and Wolfgang Iser, is based on the idea that the meaning of a text

doesn't lie hidden in the text, but is rather a product of the act of reading. Here is Iser insisting on the reader as a co-producer of the text (I quote the German version of the text because Iser seems to find the most poignant formulations when he uses his native tongue; for an English version of the text, see Iser 1971):

> Zugleich wird man sagen müssen, dass ein Text überhaupt erst zum Leben erwacht, wenn er gelesen wird. Daraus ergibt sich die Notwendigkeit, die Entfaltung des Textes durch die Lektüre zu betrachten (Iser 1988: 228).

From this discovery of the need to investigate the way in which the text unfolds in the process of reading, there is only a short step to contesting the idea that the meaning of a text is inherent in the textual structure itself. Iser immediately takes this step:

> Ein Text, so sagt man, stelle doch etwas dar, und die Bedeutung des Dargestellten existiere unabhängig von den verschiedenartigsten Reaktionen, die eine solche Bedeutung auszulösen vermag. Demgegenüber sei jedoch hier schon der Verdacht geäussert, dass die scheinbar von jeder Aktualisierung des Textes so unabhängige Bedeutung ihrerseits vielleicht nichts weiter ist als eine bestimmte Realisierung des Textes, die nun allerdings mit dem Text identifiziert ist (Iser 1988: 229).

Eco makes the point a little differently, but uses words to the same effect:

> The text is an object that the interpretation builds up in the course of the circular effort of validating itself on the basis of what it makes up as its result (Eco 1988: 162).

As can be seen from these quotations, Iser and Eco are not only making a transfer of authority from the text to the reader. They are also introducing temporality into the game of interpretation. As they insist that the text is actualised in the very act of reading, meaning becomes procedural.

2) Post-structuralism is another obvious example of the criticism of the classical idea of the work of art. In the idea of the text as a rhizome posited by Gilles Deleuze and Félix Guattari, for instance, there is indeed a temporalisation of the work of art and a blurring of its delimitations at work.

Deleuze and Guattari distinguish the rhizome-text from the classical type of text known by them as the root-book. The problem with seeing the book in terms of a tap-root is that this image abides by the "law of the One that becomes two" (Deleuze and Guattari 1987: 5). In this image of the book it becomes an organic signifying system serving as representation. Whether, on the side of the object, it is referred to nature or, on the side of the subject, it is referred to the intentions of an author, it is always seen as a derivation of an original. According to Deleuze and Guattari, a radicalisation of former attacks on this view of the text is needed if we are to overcome tradition. In many attacks the deracination hasn't gone far enough in so far as the image of the root-book has only given way to an image of the book as a radicle-system. Even if a book by, say, James Joyce shatters the linear unity of the classical book, it only does so in order to evoke a new and higher type of unity: a chaosmos instead of the root-cosmos. The rhizome, by contrast, offers a model that helps us escape all this. The rhizome-book is a text based on multiplicity. It has left the paradigm of representation behind. It is the writing of the n-1 – "the only way the one belongs to the multiple: always subtracted" (Deleuze and Guattari 1987: 6). It is an asignifying system which combines various dimensions which are multiplicities themselves already. Instead of representing the world, it produces a rhizome together with it.

As the two writers' focus is on the attempt to break away from the paradigm of representation, they emphasise the sheer exteriority of the rhizome-text. In such a book there is nothing to be interpreted. There is no semantics hiding behind the form, no subjective intentions to be discerned, no referent to be unravelled. What you see is what you get. No more, no less – pure exteriority without interiority. It is obvious, however, that they are ultimately interested in temporalising the notion of the text. A rhizome "is composed not of units, but of dimensions, or rather *directions in motion*", they insist:

> When a multiplicity of this kind changes dimension, it necessarily changes in nature as well, *undergoes a metamorphosis.* Unlike a structure, which is defined by a set of points and positions, with binary relations between the points and biunivocal relationships between the positions, the rhizome is made only of lines: lines of segmentarity and stratification as its dimensions, but also lines of flight or deterritorialisation as the maximal dimension by which, following it, *the multiplicity undergoes a metamorphosis while changing its nature* (Deleuze and Guattari 1987: 21, my italics, translation modified).

Describing the text as submitted to directions in motion and consisting of lines of flight by which the text itself undergoes a metamorphosis while changing its nature implies that temporality becomes the core element of the text. Furthermore, substituting the root-book for an image of the book as a rhizome implies an invitation to the reader to become part of a mutual transformation. If, as Deleuze and Guattari say, any point in a rhizome may, or even should, be connected to any other, there can be no privileged way of accessing the book: "Perhaps one of the most important characteristics of the rhizome is that it always has multiple entryways" (Deleuze and Guattari 1987: 12). As a consequence, the reader may choose whatever entryway he or she may like and investigate what multiplicities become visible from here. The reader must take part in the rhizomatic formation of the text, as it were, in much the same way as the text has to make a rhizome with the surrounding world.

3) In neo-pragmatism, most notably known from Stanley Fish and Richard Rorty, the text has almost disappeared in a radical form of contextualism. "Is there a text in this classroom?", Fish asks in his famous book bearing that name. The question is, of course, rhetorical. For Fish there is no text in the classroom – if by a text we understand an entity with a stable identity that guarantees its meaning once and for all. Instead there is an interpretive community which endows the

text with a particular meaning (that is, if the students agree on an interpretation) or several interpretive communities struggling to convince each other of the correctness of their interpretations (if the students tend to disagree on how a text should be read).

It is interesting to note that Fish actually means to conjure away relativism by introducing the idea of a contextualised meaning. As any interpreter is always situated in a particular context, it is, according to Fish, impossible to say very many different things about a text:

> In other words, while relativism is a position one can entertain, it is not a position one can occupy. No one can be a relativist, because no one can achieve the distance from his own beliefs and assumptions which would result in their being no more authoritative *for him* than the beliefs and assumptions held by others, or, for that matter, the beliefs and assumptions he himself used to hold (Fish 1980: 319).

Thus, the stability of interpretation has simply been moved from the text to the horizon of the reader. Rorty would hardly disagree with Fish on this point, but he is less concerned with finding counterarguments against the charge of relativism. Apparently unimpressed by the complaint, he insists that any interpretation is in fact a way of using the text for some purpose or another by a reader:

> Interpreting something, knowing it, penetrating to its essence, are all just various ways of describing some process of putting it to work (Rorty 1990: 93).

But even if Fish is right that, *in practice,* our way of using texts are restricted by the limits set up by the interpretive community to which we belong (which he probably is), it doesn't change the neo-pragmatist tenor of the argument that he shares with Rorty. In both Fish and Rorty, the text is no longer conceived as a carrier of an interior meaning to be disclosed by the reader. It is rather seen as an occasion for ever changing interpreters, or for members of various interpretive communities, to formulate their views on whatever. The emphasis has clearly swung from the text to the reader and, furthermore, the meaning has become ephemeral, as it will inevitably change with the change of the interpretational needs of the different readers using the text.

I realise that my introduction to the three positions is rather sketchy, but I hope it will suffice in order to make plausible my claim that the classical notion of the work of art has been attacked with the help of an insistence on temporality and recipient participation. For the sake of compatibility I have only chosen examples from the field of literary theory. In passing, I would like to mention that a similar tendency to transgress our classical understanding of the work of art could fairly easily be demonstrated in other branches of aesthetic theory. Theory on theatre, for instance, has begun to focus on the performative dimension. With this shift in concern theoreticians have focused on the fact that a theatre production is first and foremost characterised by taking place here and now, i.e. that it is temporal and dependent on the reactions of the spectators who are co-present with the actors and influencing their performance. Erika Fischer-Lichte's attempt to develop an *Ästhetik des Performativen* is a poignant example of this trend (cf. Fischer-Lichte 2004). Likewise, in the theory on the visual arts we have witnessed a tendency to think in terms of entryways into the works of art and the temporality of reception. In fact, scholars in this field seem to have taken their lead from the performative turn in the theory of theatre. (For an account of this tendency in the area of the visual arts, see Jalving 2005).

The general point I am trying to make is, however, that if the presented criticism is feasible, it seems hard to maintain a classical notion of the work of art according to which it is a self-contained entity, a coherent whole with an inherent meaning which may be determined once and for all. If this is so – and for the sake of argument let us assume that it is – it seems reasonable to ask: Can't we just let go of the obsolete notion of the work of art? Tempting as this attitude may be, I am afraid that it is not that easy. As soon as we ask by what the classical concept should be replaced, we seem to be in trouble. Asking this question lets us beware of the fact that a version of the classical concept seems to return in the positions held by writers who work hard to discard it.

The return of the classical concept of the work of art

The difficulties inherent in scrapping the work of art have often been debated in relation to the legacy of the so-called historical avant-garde. If, as for instance argued by Peter Bürger (1974), the historical avant-garde was all about overcoming the separation between art and life practice by transforming the work of art into an event of reality, then, as Bürger also argues, the avant-garde failed. Even Duchamp's famous urinal became, in time, a work of art that is now presented at museums of fine art; even Artaud, in spite of his attempt to avoid repeating himself in the form of a work of art by turning art into a festival of non-repetition, couldn't help leaving traces; and even Yves Klein's attempt to stage the act of painting by letting his models do the painting themselves with the use of their naked bodies became a masterpiece of the Fluxus movement. As far as I can see, it is possible to demonstrate a similar trait in the positions based on an attempt to escape the classical conception of the work of art. I shall try to show how the positions from the field of literary theory which I have already introduced seem to be shipwrecked on the shores of classical thinking after all. I shall begin with the aesthetics of reception.

As a matter of fact, Eco has found it necessary to defend the classical notion of the work of art based on the idea of coherence. This may seem a little surprising: Hasn't Eco been so keen on getting at "the role of the reader" that he has written an entire book bearing this very title? And hasn't he taken a particular interest in what he, in *Opera aperta*, has called "a work in motion" – a form of art which is directly dependent on the *physical* intervention of the recipient (cf. Eco 1981)? But even if the move may seem surprising, in a series of lectures under the heading "Interpretation and overinterpretation" he nevertheless joins the worried group of theoreticians who are concerned by the relativistic attitude that seems to result from reader-oriented positions such as deconstruction and neo-pragmatism. In the light of such positions he finds it necessary to defend the 'rights' of the text.

He launches his attack with the help of a distinction between *intentio auctoris, intentio operis,* and *intentio lectoris,* i.e. between the intentions of the author, of the text itself, and of the reader. With the help of this distinction he wants to exclude the author as well as the reader as potential referents for an interpretation. Regarding the role of the author's intentions, he follows the traditions inaugurated by the theoreticians of the so-called New Criticism. Being a writer himself, he feels tempted to defend the rights of the author, but he finally decides against it. "I hope my listeners will agree", he concludes, "that I have introduced the empirical author in this game only in order to stress his irrelevance and to reassert the rights of the text" (Eco 1992b: 84). Thus, he refrains from securing the meaning of the text by referring it to what the author allegedly means. On the other hand, and more important for my discussion, he wants to disclaim the rights of the reader. For this purpose he needs the distinction between interpretation and use that Rorty does his best to undo. Eco finds it legitimate to use a text for whatever personal purpose (like, for instance, backing up a belief by quoting a particular fictive character), but he doesn't want this way of dealing with texts to be called interpretation. If we wish to make an interpretation, Eco believes we must accept to let the text play the upper hand. A valid interpretation and a true understanding of the *intentio operis* can only be reached by following the paths that are laid out by the textual strategies.

As Rorty has argued, this line of reasoning almost takes Eco back to a position à la E. D. Hirsch who makes a distinction between "meaning and significance – a distinction between getting inside the text itself and relating the text to something else" (Rorty 1990: 93). Eco is, however, still struggling with the problem of the role of the reader, and for solving this problem he comes up with the idea of a *model reader* who, as part of the internal semiotic strategies of the text, is supposed to be a counterpart to *the model author* of the text:

A text can foresee a model reader entitled to try infinite conjectures. The empirical reader is only an actor who makes conjectures about the kind of model reader postulated by the text. Since the intention of the text is basically to produce a model reader able to make conjectures about it, the initiative of the model reader consists in figuring out a model author that is not the empirical one and that, in the end, coincides with the intention of the text (Eco 1992a: 64).

If read carefully, this passage is very revealing. The distinction between an empirical and a model author seems to be clear-cut. The real author is out of the picture. Dealing with the model author, simply means figuring out what the *intentio operis* may be. On the side of the reader, however, the distinction becomes blurred. It is obvious that Eco wants to establish a similar distinction between an empirical and a non-empirical implicit reader. The former is the actual reader who makes conjectures about the meaning of the text; the latter is an implied model reader who is created by the text itself and thus functions as a privileged gateway to the text that should be used by the real reader. But in the second half of the quotation the model reader takes on another meaning. Here, it seems to refer to a particular *empirical* reader. All of a sudden, Eco talks about the reasonable *real* reader who accepts to (actively as it were) take on the passive role of figuring out what the *implied* (as opposed to the *empirical*) model author has in mind.

Attempting to become a model reader of Eco's texts, I would like to offer the following conjecture regarding the reasons for the surprising conceptual fuzziness. Eco, himself, believes that he is "trying to keep a dialectical link between *intentio operis* and *intentio lectoris*" (ibid.), but I am not sure that this self-description gives an accurate account of what is at stake. In spite of his hermeneutical confession, Eco rather seems interested in conflating the understanding of the real reader with the understanding 'possessed by' the model reader in the text. The immediate objective is obvious. Eco's key aim is to keep the reader in his or her proper place as a passive interpreter. For this purpose, however, he doesn't need a dialectics between message and recipient. He is, on the contrary, forced to argue in two directions at the same time. On the one hand, he needs a strict distinction between the text and the reader. The text must be awarded a voice of its own that cannot be altered by the reader. But on the other hand, he needs to entertain the idea that it is possible for the actual reader to become identical with the implied model reader. Without this possibility it would be impossible to sustain the distinction between interpretation and overinterpretation (or use) because we would never know whether we have hit bedrock. Thus, he needs the distinction and, at the same time, he needs it to disappear. What is needed is, in other words, a distinction that is simultaneously strict and blurred.

There is no doubt in my mind that Eco offers a valuable sophistication of traditional hermeneutics, but my point is that the offer is based on very classical grounds. Actually, I believe that the analysis of the double need of drawing a distinction and blurring it may be extended to any position that sticks to a classical view of communication. As long as the process of communication is understood as a transmission of meaning from one position to the next, the duplicity seems unavoidable. It simply doesn't seem possible to maintain the understanding of communication as a one way street ending with a passive recipient without the simultaneous drawing and blurring of the distinction between message and receiver. It is no wonder, then, that Eco closes the discussion by embedding his belief in the possibility of a true interpretation in a very classical view of the text. Wondering how to prove a conjecture about the *intentio operis* made by an empirical reader, Eco insists:

> The only way is to check it upon the text *as a coherent whole.* This idea, too, is an old one and comes from Augustine (De doctrina christiana): any interpretation given of a certain portion of a text can be accepted if it is confirmed by, and must be rejected if it is challenged by, another portion of the same text. In this sense *the internal coherence* controls the otherwise uncontrollable drives of the reader (Eco 1992a: 65, my italics).

Here, we have reached the heart of Eco's argument. His distinction between interpreting and using texts (or between interpretation and overinterpretation) is only tenable in so far as the singular text is conceived as a coherent whole. His entire argument rests on the very formula that I used in order to characterise the traditional view of the work of art. To Eco, the physical limit of the text determines the limits of interpretation.

Now, let us take a brief look at Iser's version of the aesthetics of reception and ask whether he is more successful in overcoming the traditional concept of the work of art. Compared to Eco, Iser seems to stay more focused on the role of the *real* reader in the process of making sense of a text. But even if this is so, his argument still seems to end with a return to the holistic concept of the work of art. From the outset, Iser is far more radical than Eco. He opens with a very polemical remark which, even if no names are mentioned, seems to be directly aimed at Schleiermacher and the hermeneutical tradition:

> Wenn es wirklich so wäre, wie uns die 'Kunst der Interpretation' glauben machen möchte, dass die Bedeutung im Text selbst verborgen ist, so fragt es sich, warum Texte mit den Interpreten solche Versteckspiele veranstalten; mehr noch aber, warum sich einmal gefundene Bedeutungen wieder verändern, obgleich doch Buchstaben, Wörter und Sätze des Textes dieselben bleiben. Beginnt da nicht eine nach dem Hintersinn der Texte fragende Interpretationsweise diese zu mystifizieren und damit ihr erklärtes Ziel, Klarheit und Licht in die Texte zu tragen, selbst wieder aufzuheben? (Iser 1988: 229).

The question posed at the ending of the quotation is obviously rhetorical. As Iser believes that the meaning of a text is, in fact, generated in the process of reading, the idea of a meaning inherent in the text (of an *intentio operis*, as it were) becomes unacceptable. In comparison to Eco, Iser seems ready to accept a real dialectical relationship between text and reader. From Roman Ingarden he picks up the idea of "schematisierten Ansichten" and "Leerstellen", i.e. of images produced by the fictional framework and empty spaces that appear when two images are thrown into a relation to each other which isn't discursively evident. The idea is that the text produces empty spaces, gaps, which must be filled by the reader if he or she is to make sense of the text.

With this theoretical setup Iser means to make way for thinking meaning in terms of a co-operation performed by the text and the reader. In the passages in which Iser qualifies the dialectics, however, it becomes obvious that we are dealing with a rather asymmetrical form of dialectics in so far as the text is in fact always thought as the determining factor in the production of meaning. At one place Iser tries to open the text towards the reader:

> Nun ist zwar die in der Lektüre sich einstellende Bedeutung vom Text *konditioniert*, allerdings in einer Form, die es erlaubt, dass sie der Leser selbst erzeugt (Iser 1988: 249, my italics).

Here, Iser obviously tries to downgrade the role of the text while upgrading the role of the reader. It is the reader who actualises the meaning. In spite of this, it becomes clear that it is the text that has got the power to condition the reading. Even if the reader is playing an active role, it is still a fact that "dennoch muss der Text *die Bedingungen für* die unterschiedliche Realisierungen erhalten", as he puts it elsewhere (Iser 1988: 235, my italics). He even insists that the text takes control over the reactions of the reader:

> So bewirkt diese Struktur zum einen die Beteiligung des Lesers an der Bewertung, zum anderen aber *die Kontrolle* derjenigen Reaktionen, denen die Bewertung entspringt (Iser 1988: 240, my italics).

With these remarks Iser parts with the pragmatist tenor of his initial argument about the activity of the reader and returns to a position very close to Eco's. Even if the real reader is supposed to play a vital part in the production of meaning, his or her activity is only thought of in terms of a participation in an excavation of textual meaning. Also in Iser, the reader is submitted to the control performed by the text. This return to the idea of the text as the origin of meaning inevitably seems to evoke the classical organic notion of the work of art. Unlike Eco, Iser doesn't explicitly reinvest in the idea of coherence as an explanation of how the control is performed by the text. It is, however, obvious that what he calls "die Appellstruktur der Texte" is but another name for it. As far as I can see, it only makes sense to talk about such a structure if it is understood as the way in which the text *as a coherent entity* appeals to the reader. Thus, the structure of appeal is simply a reader oriented version of the notion of totality.

Perhaps it is not so surprising, after all, that a classical view of the text is at work in Eco and Iser. Their branch of the aesthetics of reception (no less than the other branch represented by Hans Rupert Jauss and Hans Georg Gadamer, by the way) is probably best understood as an attempt to develop a strategy of interpretation which is meant to be a sophistication of classical hermeneutics rather than a complete dismissal of it. But what happens in post-structuralism whose defenders tend to see themselves as being at odds with the entire tradition of interpretation – at least as it appears in the West, be it in the form of semiotics, structuralism, hermeneutics and so on and so forth.

Taking Deleuze and Guattari as our example, it would be unfair to say that nothing has happened. Indeed, the view of the text as well as the understanding of the relationship between the text and the reader have changed dramatically. From time to time, Deleuze and Guattari may actually sound almost neo-pragmatist. In a passage from the original (untranslated) version of their text about the rhizome from 1976 that, interestingly enough, has been omitted in *Mille plateaux* in which most of the original text has been re-used as an introduction, they use formulations that Rorty could easily have employed:

> Le livre a cessé d'être un microcosme, à la manière classique, ou à la manière européenne. Le livre n'est pas une image du monde, encore moins un signifiant. Ce n'est pas une belle totalité organique, ce n'est pas non plus une unité de sens. Quand on demande à Michel Foucault ce qu'un livre est pour lui, il répond: c'est une boîte à outils. [...] il n'y a pas de mort du livre, mais une autre manière de lire. *Dans un livre il n'y a rien à comprendre, mais beaucoup à se servir.* Rien à i interpreter ni à signifier, mais beaucoup à expérimenter (Deleuze and Guattari 1976: 72, my italics).

The closeness to neo-pragmatism is stunning. Even though Deleuze and Guattari assure us that there is no death of the book, it seems to have vanished into a maze of arbitrary uses to which various readers may have chosen to put it. "Prenez ce que vous voulez", is the pragmatist credo by which the authors seem to break completely with the idea of the text as a totality to be investigated by a subordinate reader (ibid.).

Rorty and Fish would have relished these lines. However, it may very well be indicative that exactly this passage wasn't allowed to remain in the remake of the text in *Mille plateaux*. As opposed to Rorty and Fish, Deleuze and Guattari do not, in fact, want to licence any use of the text. Using texts as toolboxes doesn't really mean finding different means for various purposes. In the end, they actually only seem to have one legitimate purpose in mind. To them, you only become truly pragmatic in so far as you move in the direction of multiplicity. Why? Because multiplicity is what life is considered to be fundamentally about. What I am getting at is, of course, the fact that there seems to be an ontology lurking in the background of the rhizomatic pragmatics proposed by Deleuze and Guattari – an ontology that takes its lead from Bergson (for an account of the central Bergsonian inspiration, see, for instance, Hardt 1993). This ontology of multiplicity seems to make them reterritorialise unnecessarily on classical grounds.

A passage in which they distinguish between the book as a *spiritual* reality (comme réalité spirituelle) and the book as a *natural* reality (comme réalité naturelle) is particularly revealing in this respect:

One that becomes two: whenever we encounter this formula [...] what we have before us is the most classical and well reflected, oldest, and weariest kind of thought. Nature doesn't work in that way: in nature, roots are taproots with a more multiple, lateral, and circular system of ramification, rather than a dichotomous one. *Thought lags behind nature.* Even the book as a natural reality is a taproot, with its pivotal spine and surrounding leaves (Deleuze and Guattari 1980: 5, my italics).

It is difficult to overlook the double ontologisation in this quotation. If thought lags behind nature, it is because it gets stuck in the metaphysical habits of arborescent thinking. By consequence, it is incapable of 'living up to' the true multiplicity of nature. Indeed, the Platonic formula has been inversed. Nature isn't a stable being that may work as a secure reference for the interpretation of the world anymore. Nevertheless, defining it as a heterogeneous multiplicity in constant flux is still an ontological gesture. Likewise, the distinction between the book as a spiritual and as a natural reality implies an ontology of the book. Taking it in the first sense means misunderstanding what actually goes on in a book. By, contrast, conceiving it as a natural reality means getting it right. It means realising that it is, in fact, a heterogeneous assemblage. With the application of this distinction the rhizome is no longer the image of a particular book which must be opposed to the root- and the radicle-book; instead it becomes the image of what, according to Deleuze and Guattari, a book really is.

Substituting an ever changing multiplicity for the view of life as an ordered totality and a proliferating rhizome for the organic view of the text does make a difference, as it were. No doubt about that. Nevertheless, I find it fair to say that, in spite of Deleuze's and Guattari's insistence that there is no central reference controlling a rhizome, the idea of multiplicity as the 'essence' of life pretty much works as if it was in fact such a reference. In so far as everything must be turned towards multiplicity, we are heading dangerously towards a renewed understanding of the book as a form of representation. As multiplicities in themselves, texts refer to the multiplicity of nature while the readers, in turn, must follow the multiplicity of the text by making a rhizome with it.

Now, there is no reason to make the point more polemical than need be. Thus, it should be added that we are probably dealing with a *re-creation* rather than a *re-presentation* of multiplicity. The rhizomatic texts do not actually produce an image of a multiplicity which is 'out there'. Instead they produce a multiplicity of their own and *thereby* bear witness to the overall heterogeneous nature of life. The same goes for the relation between text and reader. The reader is not supposed to reiterate the multiplicity of the book in the form of a redoubling commentary, but is rather asked to 'hook up' into the particular multiplicity produced by the book in order to follow it on a line of flight away from habitual arborescent thinking. This idea of texts as recreations rather than representations of multiplicity may in fact explain why Deleuze and Guattari insist on seeing themselves as pragmatists. To them, there is no real difference between writing and reading. Reading is as active an act as writing because it is involved in the same process of recreation. The decisive demarcation line goes between partaking in the *creation* of life and having capitulated to an arborescent *interpretation* of it.

Still, it seems reasonable to wonder whether Deleuze's and Guattari's presentation of themselves as pragmatists is, in fact, a valid self-description. In so far as there is only one problem to be solved, only one direction in which we must direct ourselves, and only one acceptable interpretation of reality towards which texts and readers alike must point, we seem to be back on a well-known metaphysical track. Even if the text is, indeed, no longer conceived as "une belle totalité organique", it still seems to be ordered by the central idea of becoming-multiple. For the reader there seems to be more to understand in the rhizomatic text than Deleuze and Guattari, when in the pragmatist mood, are ready to admit. Apparently 'real' or even 'true' texts are those that reveal the fundamental heterogeneity of life.

One way to describe the transgression of, yet closeness to the tradition of metaphysics in Deleuze and Guattari is to borrow a formula used by Jean-François Lyotard for determining what goes on in the avant-garde art in the twentieth century. Speaking of Barnett Newman's paintings as a poignant example of the avant-garde tradition, he concludes:

[...] Newman judged surrealism to be over-reliant on a pre-romantic or romantic approach to indeterminacy. Thus, when he seeks sublimity in the here and now he breaks with the eloquence of romantic art *but he does not reject the fundamental task, that of bearing witness to the inexpressible* (Lyotard 1991: 199, my italics).

129

In so far as Lyotard is right about this, post-structuralist theory like that of Deleuze's and Guattari seems to stand in pretty much the same relation to classical theory as avant-garde art relates to classical art. It not only transgresses the aesthetics of beauty based on notions like harmonious form and organic unity by taking an aesthetics of the sublime turned towards the ineffable aboard; it even transgresses the romanticist version of the sublime. *But,* and in this connection this is the most important point, it also maintains the programme of the sublime, even if it happens in a manner that transforms the original conception of the sublime.

It should be noted, however, that Deleuze and Guattari explicitly rule against this interpretation. In a passage that appears to be an indirect dialogue with Romanticists like Friedrich Schlegel and Novalis, they say that we may need "anexact expressions" in order to "designate something exactly", but that this has got nothing to do with an approximation:

> The problem of writing: in order to designate something exactly, anexact expressions are utterly unavoidable. Not at all because it is a necessary step, or because one can only advance by approximations: anexactitude is in no way an approximation; on the contrary it is the exact passage of that which is under way. We evoke one dualism only in order to challenge another. We employ a dualism of models only in order to arrive at a process that challenges all models. *It is up to the reader to have the necessary mental correctives that undo the dualisms* we had no wish to construct but through which we pass (Deleuze and Guattari 1980: 20, translation modified, my italics).

With this remark they clearly want to set themselves apart from the tradition of the sublime. The anexact expressions they use shouldn't be seen as part of what Manfred Frank, in an exposé of early romanticist philosophy, has called "eine unendliche Annäherung" (cf. Frank 1997). Instead they want us to conceive them as means that shouldn't be taken too seriously. Apparently, they bet on the reader's ability to correct the inadequacy of language in their minds. It is up to the reader to make the necessary cerebral corrections when trying to understand what the non-approximations really mean.

I believe that I am actually capable of making the cerebral corrections that Deleuze and Guattari want me to. It actually seems possible to 'read between the lines'. In the framework of mind set up by Deleuze and Guattari, however, this solution as to how we may avoid the idea of anexact expressions as approximations is rather surprising. Not only does it seem to be at odds with the idea that there is nothing but exteriority in a rhizome-text. If there is nothing 'behind' the text, how can it be possible to penetrate to an understanding of the 'real' content of an anexact expression? And if there is no interiority in a word, a concept, or an image, by which mental powers should the penetration be made? Can multiplicity be detected via a mental endeavour that has not yet fallen prey to the exteriority of language, after all? Furthermore, the idea of leaving it up to the reader to correct the inevitable drawbacks of the text also seems to undermine the invitation to stop interpreting texts. For don't they ask us here to interpret their text in order to look behind the treacherous language they use? I simply fail to see that the claim that the cerebral corrections may be made by the reader can make sense without a reference to an approximation to the inexpressibly sublime. Thus, even the manoeuvre Deleuze and Guattari use in order to get rid of the tradition of the sublime seems to lead right back to it. After all, rhizomatics apparently is all about bearing witness to multiplicity and the rhizome-text – for all its lines of flights and deterritorialisations – is considered to be the (self-undermining) entity that is suitably equipped for doing the trick.

Now, finally, we must turn to neo-pragmatism which may be dealt with a little more hastily: The position defended by Fish and Rorty strikes me as being at the same time very radical and very traditional. On the one hand, neo-pragmatism probably gets as close to giving up the concept of the work of art as can be. If reading texts means putting them to whatever use you may like, the idea of a self-contained text controlling the reading doesn't make any sense. The proof of the pudding is not even in the eating. In neo-pragmatism there is only eating. *In practice,* on the other hand, there is nothing radical about neo-pragmatism at all. Fish and Rorty both proceed as representatives of classical hermeneutics trying to wrench the meaning from the texts they happen to read.

It is true, however, that the rationale for respecting the totality of the text is very non-hermeneutical. In Rorty's wording, a neo-pragmatist views

> [...] the imperative to check your interpretation against the text as a coherent whole simply as a reminder that, *if you want to make your interpretation of a book sound plausible,* you cannot just gloss one or two lines or scenes. You have to say something about what most of the other lines or scenes are doing there (Rorty 1992: 95, first italics added).

Thus, a neo-pragmatist only takes the idea of the text as a coherent whole seriously in order to become equipped for participating in the power game of interpretation. But even if Fish and Rorty have only pragmatic reasons for accepting the notion of totality, they nevertheless proceed reading along the lines evoked by, for instance, Eco. Consequently, in dealing with neo-pragmatism you seem to be faced with a choice between two options. You can either go with the radical things neo-pragmatists *say*, leave behind the worry about saying something true about texts and begin using them for developing values we may live by instead. Or you may take them seriously as pragmatists and go with the rather ordinary interpretational manoeuvres that they *make*. It should be realised, however, that both options are ripe with consequences. Grabbing the first horn would, of course, imply skipping the theoretical enterprise altogether whereas betting on the latter possibility would take you right back to square one because, in practice, it implies a reinstatement of the classical work of art.

At this point I would like to sum up the argument I have presented so far. If I am correct that a) the classical concept of the work of art as a self-contained and coherent whole has become difficult to maintain in the light of the heavy criticism of it; that b) a classical concept of the work of art – or various substitutions for it – tends to reappear in positions that aim at transgressing it; and that c) the only way of ridding ourselves of the classical concept is to let go of the theoretical project of getting it right – if I am not mistaken in all of this, then we seem to be faced with a choice between two alternatives: We may either become happy-go-lucky neo-pragmatists and disregard any theoretical ambition altogether or we may, if we want to stay on the theoretical track, start looking for a third way to define the work of art – a way that must be found somewhere in between the classical concept and the dismissal of it. Though I have a lot of sympathy for the 'cut the crap' attitude inherent in the neo-pragmatist solution, I shall not go down that road. Here I am, as a matter of fact, struggling to find a theoretical solution to the impasse based on the double impossibility we seem to be facing (i.e. the simultaneous impossibility of maintaining the classical work of art and the impossibility of getting rid of it). For this purpose the neo-pragmatist rejection of theory is hardly an option. Instead I am left with the latter possibility and I must therefore now turn to the question of how we may formulate a third view of the work of art.

Before I begin this undertaking, however, I would like to specify the direction in which I think we should look. Talking about 'a third way' may seem to imply a *dialectical* approach, i.e. a solution which is supposed to mediate between the classical insistence on totality and the attempt to transgress it. As I tend to find the post-structuralist criticism of dialectics rather appropriate, however, I believe that the solution should be found in a theoretical framework that disregards dialectics. A dialectical solution to problems like the one I have pointed out tends to fail because the alleged mediation always seems to suffer from the flaw of thinking 'the other' in terms of negativity. As post-structuralists never become weary of pointing out, the so-called mediations of dialectical solutions are always inaugurated from one of the two initial positions and, by consequence, not very dialectical after all. As Guattari and Deleuze put it, dialectics is also always operating with a major and a minor. Or, if phrased in a wording borrowed from Derrida, even in dialectics a hierarchical dichotomy is controlling the discourse. For this reason I tend to favour non-dialectical solutions and for the purpose of getting at such a solution a theoretical framework based on a thought of difference seems to be needed.

I have dedicated the remainder of my contribution to an elaboration of the un-dialectical approach. I shall begin by investigating the deconstructivist view. Dissatisfied with the answers to be found in the deconstructivist framework of mind, however, I am going to suggest, in the final section of the article, that we may benefit more from searching for theoretical backup in a constructivist version of systems theory than from sticking to deconstruction. As I am searching for a theory based on a philosophy of difference, I have chosen Niklas Luhmann for my interlocutor in this section. But first a brief look at what is offered by deconstruction in order to make plausible my suggestion that we attempt to transgress it.

Deconstruction between inevitable and unnecessary metaphysics

I have a very particular reason for starting out with an investigation of deconstruction. My redescription of the problem concerning the definition of the work of art is, in fact, pretty much informed by deconstructivist reasoning. The Derridean inspiration of my way of construing an image of the situation is probably obvious. The double thesis – that neither the attempt to uphold a classical conception of the work of art nor the attempt to transgress it seem successful – owes a lot to Derrida's approach to metaphysics in general. On the one hand, Derrida regards metaphysics as a self-undermining illusion that ought to be left behind. In spite of his extensive investigation of the criticism of metaphysics, on the other hand, he cannot seem to find any trustworthy formulation of a real 'beyond' and consequently he concludes that (at least as yet) it seems impossible to escape from the prison house of metaphysics. (For an elaboration of this view of Derridean deconstruction, see Lehmann 1994.) Indeed, my duplicity is not only indebted *structurally* to Derrida; it is actually deeply imbedded in the dual front opened by him. Thus, it only seems possible to come up with an alternative to the classical notion of the work of art if we leave the realm of metaphysical thinking, but the non-metaphysical alternative is apparently hard to come by because the metaphysical concept of the work of art always seems to sneak in by the backdoor.

Derrida contends that the double condition posed by the fact that we can neither rely on metaphysics nor rejoice in overcoming it leaves us only one option. According to him we can only be situated in the margins of philosophy – a position which is neither completely inside nor totally outside the metaphysics governing philosophy. Indeed, if Derrida is not mistaken in his analyses of the metaphysical and anti-metaphysical positions from Plato to Heidegger and onwards, this is an inevitable conclusion. The question is, however, whether the deconstructivist idea of what it may mean to stay in the margins of philosophy is as cogent as the analysis of our predicament. I am not quite convinced that it is. In order to show why, I need to build an argument based on a particular distinction. In dealing with attempts to transgress the horizon of metaphysics it may be advantageous to draw a distinction between *necessary*, unavoidable reintroductions of metaphysical concepts, on the one hand, and *unnecessary* relapses into metaphysical habits of thinking, on the other.

With the introduction of this distinction I take my lead from Rorty, who has used it several times in order to distinguish between different forms of deconstruction. At one place he argues in favour of a distinction between the early, still too metaphysical Derrida and the late Derrida, who has given up his youthful dreams of getting right what Heidegger couldn't (cf. Rorty 1989). In a later piece of writing he makes a similar distinction, but now he suggests that the demarcation line goes between the methodological form of deconstruction known from the application of deconstruction in the field of literary theory, on the one hand, and the philosophical enterprise of Derrida on the other (cf. Rorty 1991). In the eyes of Rorty the former is unnecessarily metaphysical, whereas he sees the latter as a non-metaphysical stance with which he would like to team up. I shall leave the intriguing question whether Rorty hits the spot with one or the other distinction unanswered. (My guess is that both hypotheses are incorrect because the distinction to be made is rather between two opposing tendencies in the texts produced by the various deconstructors, including both early and late Derrida as it were.) The point of introducing Rorty's readings of deconstruction is, however, that they suggest that it makes sense to investigate different forms of deconstruction in terms of how inevitable the reemerging metaphysics is. Using this distinction as my analytical tool, I shall try to show how the three founding fathers of deconstruction seem to differ – even if they seem to say very similar things. In my opinion, J. Hillis Miller, the most classical interpreter of the three, may be seen as a deconstructivist who is tempted to become unnecessarily metaphysical. As opposed to Hillis Miller, Derrida himself is less inclined to succumbing to the temptation of metaphysics. Paul de Man, in turn, doesn't seem to be quite as cautious as Derrida, but, with respect to the distinction between inevitable and unnecessary metaphysics, his form of deconstruction seems to be closer to Derrida's position than Hillis Miller's. Let me begin with a look at Hillis Miller, who, in spite of the radicalism which is supposed to characterise his position, seems to evoke fairly classical figures of thought.

One piece of writing by Hillis Miller is particularly revealing as to his position in the theoretical landscape of deconstruction. I am thinking of the criticism he has made of Joseph Riddel, a fellow deconstructivist, in his famous article "Deconstructing the Deconstructors". For my purpose, this article is not only interesting because the need to criticise another deconstructivist forces him to be very explicit about his own views. The text is also very suitable because Hillis Miller actually raises the question whether the bits and pieces of metaphysical thinking he finds in Riddel's book on William Carlos Williams, *The Inverted Bell,* are in fact inevitable or simply the effects of bad mental habits.

In his book Riddel uses Heidegger and Derrida as a philosophical backdrop for understanding the poetry of Williams. Hillis Miller has no objections to this strategy, but he detects a certain equivocation in the argumentation. Using a distinction between Heideggerian nostalgia and Derridean freeplay of the signifier as his matrix, Riddel wants to distinguish, on the one hand, between the epoch of modernism and the era of postmodernism in order to make of Williams a postmodernist. On the other hand, however, Riddel seems to embrace the idea "that Heidegger, Derrida, Williams, and he himself are saying roughly 'the same thing'" (Hillis Miller 1975: 25). In the light of this conflation of all the positions, the distinction between modernism and postmodernism is in danger of evaporating. In this strand of the text, furthermore, Hillis Miller is capable of showing that Heidegger wins the day. The conflation does not turn Heidegger into a Derridean. It is rather a case of turning Derrida into a Heideggerian. If the distinction between the freeplay of deconstruction and the nostalgia of Heidegger (needed for the argument in favour of seeing Williams as a postmodernist) is undercut, it is because Riddel tends to embed the alleged postmodernist Williams in the modernist search for origins after all.

Having detected two contradictory strands of argument, Hillis Miller goes on to ask whether Riddel is confused "in a way which might have been clarified" or whether there is "some necessity in the deconstructive enterprise which means that it is always open in its turn to deconstruction" (Hillis Miller 1975: 29). To this question he offers a double answer. On the one hand, he believes that Riddel's book "would have been clarified if he had remained more faithful to his intermittent insight into the difference between Heidegger and Derrida" (ibid.). Riddel could, in other words, have avoided an amount of unnecessary metaphysics if he had avoided turning Derrida into a Heideggerian. On the other hand, Hillis Miller insists that

deconstructive discourse can never reach a clarity which is not vulnerable to be deconstructed in its turn. However clarified, refined, or sophisticated Riddel were to become it would still be possible to show that his work is incoherent (Hillis Miller 1975: 30).

In other words, no matter how much Riddel works on turning Williams into a post-metaphysical postmodernist, he cannot escape the metaphysics of modernism which seems to reappear in his argumentation.

Now, I do not investigate Hillis Miller's reading of Riddel's book in order to find out which of the two judgments is correct. My errand is rather to ponder whether Hillis Miller himself falls prey to the use of unnecessary metaphysical reasoning in his criticism of Riddel. In so far as he detects the problem in Riddel, it could be expected that he would be very anxious not to fall into the same trap as Riddel allegedly does. He is, however, surprisingly incautious, if not even careless in handling this problem.

Why can Hillis Miller insist that the failure of Riddel to keep his ship out of metaphysical waters is not only a product of lack of critical talent, but rather an inevitable consequence of the power of the metaphysical tradition? Because he believes that, *by necessity*, texts are heterogeneous. By the end of the article on Riddel he establishes – as a sheer fact – that

> [...] the heterogeneity of the text (and so its vulnerability to deconstruction) lies [...] in the fact that it says two entirely incompatible things at the same time. Or rather, it says something which is capable of being interpreted in two irreconcilable ways. It is 'undecidable'. One way is the referential (there is an origin), and the other the deconstruction of this referentiality (there is no origin, only the freeplay of linguistic substitution) (Hillis Miller 1975: 30).

With this definition Hillis Miller is, no doubt, pointing in the direction of a non-dialectical concept of the text of the kind that I am looking for. We are dealing with a view of the text according to which two forces are at war with each other. One side of the text is turned towards order and coherence because it is dedicated to a referent. The other side introduces an element of chaos and disorder because it allegedly undermines the referential dimension of the text. In so far as the two forces involved in the battle are irreconcilable, we are dealing with a *paradoxical* unity. My point is, however, that the view is posited, without any hesitation, as an *ontological* definition of the text as such. According to Hillis Miller, any text is apparently split between metaphysical and non-metaphysical motives. Considering the complaint he files against Riddel's failure to acknowledge the difference between Heidegger and Derrida, this view is rather surprising. Here, Hillis Miller seems to commit the same 'error' as he detects in Riddel. Indeed, the perspective has changed from Heidegger to Derrida, but the insistence on undecidability as the ontological foundation of texts threatens to eradicate the difference between metaphysical modernism and non-metaphysical postmodernism no less than Riddel's tendency to turn Derrida into Heidegger.

Perhaps it may be argued that, for the sake of argument and for strategic purposes, Hillis Miller is simply speaking the language of ontology in order to turn it against itself and that I am taking his words too much at face value. I am not convinced of the validity of this argument, though. It might have made sense to think of the ontology of the text as an 'as if' ontology if it hadn't been for an even more surprising *epistemological* remark made by Hillis Miller. "My account of deconstruction has been misleading", he says,

> [if] it has suggested that the dismantling is performed from the outside by the critic on a piece of language which remains innocently mystified about its own status. This is by no means the case. The 'unreadability' (if there is such a word) of a text is more than an experience of unease in the reader, the result of his failure to be able to reduce the text to a homogeneous reading. [...] The text performs on itself the act of deconstruction without any help from the critic (Hillis Miller 1975: 31).

This remark is surprising because it takes Hillis Miller all the way back to classical hermeneutics – or perhaps it would be more precise to say that it threatens to make him fall back to a position that is more positivistic than hermeneutical. Hillis Miller actually doesn't posit a dialectical relationship between the text and the reader, as, for instance, in the aesthetics of reception of Iser. Instead, he presents an image of the relationship according to which the reader is a passive witness who is only supposed to follow as precisely as possible what happens in the text.

It is tempting to dismiss this crucial distinction between an active text and a passive reader as a slip of the tongue in a theoretically unambitious text which is only meant as a piece of criticism. As it can be found in other writings of Hillis Miller as well, however, this solution lacks plausibility. Elsewhere, the view is reiterated. For instance: "the readings of deconstructive criticism are not the wilful imposition by a subjectivity of a theory on the texts, but are coerced by the texts themselves" (Hillis Miller 1980: 611). Thus, the classical epistemology seems to be a constant in Hillis Miller's thinking about textual analysis. In this light it seems reasonable to concede about this form of deconstruction that it should be seen as an elaboration of the heritage of New Criticism. Apparently, Hillis Miller's form of deconstruction is still a form of close reading based on an absolute respect for the text. On Hillis Miller's account, understanding the heterogeneity of the text means seeing what the text really is. His insistence on the passivity of the reader in the act of deconstruction and on the self-deconstruction of the text suggests that he is deadly serious about the proposed ontology of the text.

Hillis Miller even believes, so it seems, that there is a teleology involved in the chain of deconstructions:

> This chain is not, however, an infinite regress or a vicious circle. Each deconstruction is a version of the basic act of reading. [...] The repetition with different texts of this act or non-act of deconstruction leads to *a gradual clarification*, as the reading comes back again and again, with different texts, to the 'same' impasse (Hillis Miller 1975: 30, italics added).

It should be noted, of course, that Hillis Miller uses quotation marks around the word 'same'. This is done, no doubt, in order to suggest that we are not dealing with the self-same impasse, but only with similar versions of the impasse. As far as I can see, however, what may seem like a caution not to be caught unduly in metaphysical thinking contributes rather to the metaphysical character of the argument. To Hillis Miller the impasse reached by deconstructors when they try to leave the grounds of metaphysics and realise that they cannot is not the self-same because it is always situated *on a higher level*. Each new deconstruction – like the deconstruction Hillis Miller undertakes of Riddel's deconstruction of Williams – is apparently conceived as a contribution to the "gradual clarification" Hillis Miller talks about. It is, I take it, this belief in the ongoing project of the enlightenment that allows him, from time to time, to make a surprisingly classical criticism of Riddel. Thus, Riddel is also charged with making *distortions* of Heidegger and Derrida (a rather surprising accusation to be made by a theoretician who insists that any reading is a *mis*reading) because he doesn't take into consideration the entire corpus of their texts (also a very surprising complaint in so far as it is expressed by a theoretician who believes that orienting the reading towards "the linguistic moment of the text" implies being incapable of determining definite borderlines for the text, let alone a corpus of texts).

By now, I hope it has become evident why I tend to see Hillis Miller's position as a form of deconstruction in which much unnecessary metaphysics surfaces. It is hard to see, firstly, on which grounds a deconstructor can determine, fair and square, whether a reading is simply right or wrong. The fact that Hillis Miller feels inclined to pass judgments of this kind, however, seems to be indicative of the fact that he hasn't left the realm of metaphysics. I fail to see the necessity of this counter-intentional genuflection for the tradition of truth-finding. Secondly, I have a difficulty in realising why it should be necessary to evoke a Hegelian teleology. Not only does it seem to be directly at odds with the tragic insight of deconstruction that metaphysical thinking, alas, seems to be the condition of possibility for (Western) thought. The gradual clarification also seems to be an empty claim. Hillis Miller provides no answer to the question of how we are to make sure that we are actually dealing with a process directed at an advancing clarification. If any reading will have to end with the insight that we are faced with a duality of metaphysical and anti-metaphysical themes, it is a little difficult to see what justifies the claim that we have become any wiser with each deconstructive turn of the screw of interpretation. The postulate about an inherent teleology in the line of deconstructions is as unwarranted as it seems to be unnecessary. For a literary critic it is probably very tempting to make of deconstruction an honourable method by staging it as a strategy that allows us to get at what actually goes on in the text. Nevertheless, I cannot see, thirdly, that we are bound to evoke a classical relation between subject and object according to which the text provides everything and the reader is but a passive witness of the text's self-deconstruction. Finally, I fail to see that it is inevitable to evoke an ontology of the text. Indeed, it is necessary if you want to defend deconstruction with the help of a classical epistemology. Only in so far as texts are really self-deconstructive, is it possible to posit deconstruction as the method that gets it right at last. But the question of what makes this theory more valid than other theories of the text begs to be asked. In Hillis Miller the idea of texts as being split between closure and openness is only presented as a postulate.

It is not very difficult to realize why Hillis Miller feels the need to subordinate the reader to an ontology of the text, though. At the end of the article on Riddel he maintains that *"great works of literature* are likely to be ahead of their critics. They are there already. They have anticipated explicitly any deconstruction the critic can achieve" (Hillis Miller 1975: 31, my italics). In this remark it becomes obvious that we are dealing with yet another version of the aesthetics of the sublime. Because of the very duality which literary texts allegedly display they are believed to bear witness to the indeterminable, and therefore inexpressible, reality. Literary texts are, as Hillis Miller puts it, already there – and for the literary critic it is simply a question of catching up. In this respect, Hillis Miller also seems to be an heir of New Criticism. Not only is the idea of the self-deconstruction of the text closely related to the idea of inclusivity and of the unity of opposites which was central to the New Criticists. (In an attempt to show that deconstruction is less radical than it is often claimed, Fjord Jensen, for one, makes this point succinctly in Fjord Jensen 1987). Hillis Miller also mimes the hierarchy in the relation between literature and criticism which is established by them. If I have understood the overall (romanticist) argument of New Criticism correctly, the thought runs like this: 1) Reality is complex and therefore difficult to grasp; 2) because of its ability to work with paradoxes, literature must be privileged as a form of discourse that is capable of getting closer to reality than any other form of discourse because it alone can state indirectly what cannot be stated directly by way of clear concepts; and 3) the job of the critic is to find ways of reiterating the ineffable truth of the literary work of art – to express the ineffable by not expressing it, as it were. Thus, the ontology of the text seems to be imbedded in an overall ontology of reality and it is the hierarchical relation established between reality, text and critic that may explain why we encounter a notion of a literary text as a paradoxical unity of contradicting forces in Hillis Miller. As in New Criticism we are, however, given no cogent reasons for submitting to neither the overall ontology, nor the proposed ontology of the text. They are simply taken for granted. Consequently, it is hard to count it among the inevitable pieces of metaphysical thinking.

On the whole, my reading of Hillis Miller leads me to suggest that he points in the right direction, but reterritorialises unnecessarily on metaphysical grounds. The conception of the text as being torn by two opposing forces – one of which is turned towards order and closure whereas the other force introduces disorder and dissemination – could indeed have proven beneficial for my attempt to find a third way of conceiving the work of art. The potential disappears, however, because Hillis Miller imbeds it so heavily in a surprisingly consistent genuflection for the tradition of truthfinding. In particular, his return to the aesthetics of the sublime seems to make it unsuitable for my purposes. Hillis Miller seems to join the group of theoreticians who give the appearance of being very radical, but actually reinvest in the classical view of the text as a coherent whole (even if the totality has become paradoxical). If this is a fairly correct reading of Hillis Miller, we need to ask whether there are better attempts at staying in the margin of philosophy to be found in the tradition of deconstruction. As I believe that de Man is doing a somewhat better job at staying clear of unnecessary metaphysics, I shall now turn to his position for a short investigation. De Man is indeed more careful and hence less prone to fall prey to the almost vulgar forms of metaphysics that are used by his fellow deconstructivist. Yet he is, perhaps, too committed to the ideal of getting it right to avoid unnecessary metaphysics altogether.

In "The Resistance to Theory" de Man offers a distinct version of his well-known rhetorical programme for literary theory. For de Man the aim of this branch of theory is to define the so-called *literariness* of literature. The question to be asked is how literature works *as literature* and for de Man this implies orienting the study towards the rhetorical dimension of texts. This may sound easy, but de Man tries to reveal that the study of rhetoricity in its own right is, in fact, an extremely difficult, if not downright impossible enterprise.

The fate of structuralism illustrates the difficulties involved in getting at the rhetoric of texts very well. De Man finds theoreticians of structuralism praiseworthy because they have taken the first step towards focusing on the literariness of texts. They have done so because they have changed the focus. In structuralism it is not about asking *what* a text says; instead the interest is directed at investigating *how* it works, i.e. at finding the generalisable laws governing the singular text. Nevertheless, de Man may show that structuralists seem to get stuck in metaphysical thinking because they rely on the *trivium* that organises the century-old understanding of language which is still part of our common-sense view of language. Traditionally, rhetoric is only seen as an aid, a pedagogical supplement, to the happy marriage between grammar and logic. Crudely stated, the latter two are supposed to deal with the content of language, whereas the former is supposed to relate only to the form. Hence the idea that logic and grammar have got to do with the serious stuff whereas rhetoric is only considered an unimportant auxiliary dimension. For de Man, A. J. Greimas, for one, serves as an example of the ambivalence inherent in the structuralist branch of literary theory. In a free paraphrase of de Man's treatment of Greimas, the argument goes as follows: On the one hand, Greimas does indeed shift the interest towards the formal or rhetorical dimension of literature when he tries to pin down the structures that control textuality. In so far as the study of texts is no longer pursued in order to interpret texts, Greimas is not in business for hermeneutical reasons. Instead of determining the semantics of specific texts, he aims at determining the common formal laws governing a body of texts. On the other hand, he is still concerned with the art of decoding. Indeed the act of decoding has become formalistic, but in so far as Greimas claims to excavate the grammar to which particular groups of texts pertain, he still doesn't take rhetoric seriously *as* rhetoric. The rhetoric of the text, and hence its literariness, is still treated as something external to the core that may de deduced from it, namely the structure – i.e. the logic or the grammar – that controls the rhetoric.

Not until we reverse the priority of logic and grammar over rhetoric, so the argument goes, can we hope to arrive at an understanding of literariness as such. This inversion of the hierarchy represents, however, an enormous difficulty since the gesture of taking the rhetorical dimension seriously in its own right inevitably puts literary theory at odds with the entire tradition of metaphysics:

> Difficulties occur only when it is no longer possible to ignore the epistemological thrust of the rhetorical dimension of discourse, that is, when it is no longer possible to keep it in its place as a mere adjunct, a mere ornament within the semantic system (de Man 1986: 14).

From the discussion of the position defended by Deleuze and Guattari we already know which epistemological thrust de Man is talking about. The problem is that the concern about the literariness of texts will inevitably take us to sheer exteriority. If the rhetoric of a text is no longer seen as a derivation of a particular content, a certain grammar or a general logic, and if we are, conversely, faced with the task of deriving whatever 'content' from the rhetoric of the text, then we cannot maintain the idea that the rhetorical dimension of a text is but a container for an interior meaning. Or put a little more crudely: If referents are made by the tropes of language, not mirrored by them, truth evaporates into a play of signifiers.

For de Man, it is the link between the project aimed at understanding the literariness of texts and the challenge to metaphysics

145

posed inevitably by this project which makes it fair to conclude that the resistance to theory is of *theoretical* and not just *historical* importance. On his account, there are indeed theoreticians who resist literary theory turned towards literariness because they do not want to have their metaphysical prejudices undermined, but the problem is larger than a historically contingent resistance impersonated by allegedly conservative scholars. De Man's programme is not just threatened by the resistance to having mental habits deracinated. The real problem is that it seems to be impossible to overcome the metaphysical formulas of the *trivium*. The resistance to a theory that aims at coming to terms with the literariness of texts is, so to speak, built into the programme of taking the rhetorical dimension seriously in its own right. Why is this so? Because any attempt to pin down the rhetorical dimension will inevitably take on the form of a 'grammar'. A theory of exteriority cannot avoid proceeding, as it were, by way of turning the exteriority into a seemingly interior essence. A theory of rhetoric can only take the form of a (non-rhetorical) theory about rhetoricity which must, by necessity, betray the absolute exteriority of rhetoric. This explains why de Man has to conclude that "nothing can overcome the resistance to theory since theory *is* itself this resistance" and that, simultaneously, rhetorical readings "are theory and not theory at the same time, the universal theory of the impossibility of theory" (de Man 1986: 19). What de Man detects here, so it seems, is a piece of unavoidable metaphysical thinking. The point is very Derridean. On one hand, we have to leave the metaphysical privilege accorded to logic and grammar within the *trivium* behind, but on the other hand we have to realise that there is no way to do so.

Now, for us the question is what de Man has got to offer in terms of a view of the text. As far as I can see, the answer is that he offers us a view which is very similar to, yet very different from Hillis Miller's dual conception of the text. As in Hillis Miller we are dealing with a view of the text as heterogeneous. Also in de Man texts are seen as divided into a referential dimension and a deconstruction of this referentiality produced by the exterior side of the signifiers, i.e. the rhetorical dimension. As opposed to Hillis Miller, however, he stays clear of the direct iterations of metaphysical thinking. De Man resists temptations like insisting that texts are, in principle, self-deconstructive. He doesn't seem to have an ontology of the literary work of art to offer. Nor does he suggest that the reader can simply be regarded as a passive witness to an alleged event of deconstruction which is believed to take place in the text (even if, once in a while, you get the impression that he believes that the rhetorical dimension may be studied straightforwardly by the theoretician who has realised the need to study texts for their literariness). And most importantly, he doesn't seem to buy the aestheticism which plays a central role in Hillis Miller. De Man doesn't establish a hierarchy between art and criticism according to which art becomes a privileged form of discourse because it bears witness to the inexpressible complexity of reality. De Man is barred from falling back into these metaphysical figures of thought because of his thorough-going scepticism about the ability of language to transcend its own rhetoricity.

Still, it seems fair to ask whether de Man's position isn't resting on an element of unnecessary metaphysics which is constantly looming in the background of his theory – an element which threatens to link him to the aesthetics of the sublime after all. Perhaps, it could be argued that *a metaphysics of exteriority* pops up in his way of thinking about texts. In so far as literariness is defined as the rhetorical dimension of the text and rhetoric, in turn, is conceived as the very exteriority of the text, it may seem preposterous to accuse de Man of essentialism. Nevertheless, it could be argued that there is an inversed essentialism which is no less essentialist than its metaphysical counterpart at work in de Man. If (at least in this text) he doesn't accord any privilege to the literary text, it is because he believes that the rhetorical dimension is at work in all forms of discourse. It may be that "the rhetorical dimension of language is", as de Man puts it, "more in the foreground in literature", but even so, it is at work in all discourse (de Man 1986: 17). On the face of it, this view may seem to express a modest avoidance of turning literature into the privileged placeholder of truth, but in fact it also implies an offensive version of 'literature strikes back'. If all discourse is considered essentially rhetorical, literariness becomes a definition, not only of what literature is, but of the essence of language as such. As opposed to Hillis Miller and the entire tradition of metaphysics, de Man neither offers us an ontological definition of reality, nor does he suggest that truth may be found if the right discursive means (i.e. literature) are employed. Nevertheless, he seems to replace the ontology of being with an ontology of language. In de Man, there is no hope of obtaining an extra-linguistic truth, but apparently we may get at the truth of language, i.e. at the fact that language provides us with nothing but exteriority.

As far as I can see, this apparently essentialist understanding of language as sheer exteriority threatens to link de Man unduly to the tradition of the sublime. We are not, to be sure, dealing with exactly the same kind of sublimity as the form presented to us by tradition. In de Man, it is not a matter of expressing a non-expressible truth about being. Rather it is about bearing witness to the rhetorical dimension of language. The point is, however, that, in so far as the rhetorical dimension is considered to be inexpressible, it is still conceived in the key of sublimity. As we have seen, every attempt to pin it down will inevitably turn into a grammar and hence lose sight of the actual exteriority of the rhetorical dimension. Considered as ineffable, so it seems, the rhetorical dimension becomes the new sublime object of literature as well as of literary criticism. Furthermore, the singular (heterogeneous) text of literature – or, to be more precise: any kind of text since every text is believed to be part of the general literariness of language – is seen as an indirect expression of the ineffable. Perhaps de Man's position may be summed up by saying that the singular text is turned into a metonomy of an overall rhetoricity.

If this reading of de Man is defensible, we still seem to be lingering too much in the realm of metaphysics. I fail to see that it is absolutely necessary to replace the ontology of being with an ontology of language. Likewise, it doesn't seem inevitable to turn literariness into something very similar to a sublime object of theory which we are tragically prevented from ever reaching. It is probably true that any attempt to 'catch' the sheer exteriority of language is bound to fail in the sense that it must necessarily betray the exteriority by, metaphysically, bestowing it with an (alleged) interiority. The betrayal will, however, only look compelling in so far as it is believed that we can only fight the tradition of metaphysics by getting as close as possible to what is considered to be on the 'outside' of this tradition. If it can be demonstrated that there is another way to stay in the margins of philosophy than this – and I evidently believe that this is possible, more on that later – the insistence on the need of a heroic struggle to get at the rhetorical dimension will look more like a negative dependence on metaphysics than a halfway liberation from it. The dependence is, no doubt, only *negative* since it does seem to make a difference to let sheer exteriority take the place of absolute interiority. Still, we seem to be dealing with a dependence in so far as the sheer exteriority does, in fact, play the same role as absolute interiority does within the confines of the metaphysical tradition. Thus, from an outside point of view it looks as if the very will to transgress metaphysics by pushing our thought towards the absolute other of metaphysics produces an unnecessary relapse into metaphysics.

Now, if de Man is one up in the game of avoiding unnecessary metaphysics compared to Hillis Miller, Derrida would seem to be one better than de Man. If compared to the way in which deconstruction has been used in the field of literary criticism, the Derridean version (as Rorty has pointed out) indeed seems to be far less inclined to be caught shoplifting from the metaphysical tradition. Nevertheless, I am not quite convinced that Derrida succeeds completely in preventing the return of unnecessary pieces of metaphysics. As a matter of fact, I believe that something very similar to what I have just said about de Man may be said about Derrida. Let me expand a little on this double view of Derrida.

Derrida is notoriously (and correctly) known for his ability to make yet another turn of his argument whenever it seems to move into the vicinity of metaphysical reasoning. As he has made it his trademark to disclose the relapses into a metaphysical stance of which other anti-metaphysical positions seem to be guilty, he is of course very cautious not to fall into obvious traps like, for instance, positing an ontology of the text (let alone an ontology of language). Unlike Hillis Miller (and like de Man) he is careful not to talk about texts being self-deconstructive just as he avoids staging himself as a detective capable of revealing the deconstructive movement which is supposed to be carried out by the text itself. In fact, he is refraining completely from determining 'where' the deconstructive event takes place. His favourite strategy for avoiding to determine this issue (for keeping it undecidable, as it were) is the use of enigmatic formulas by which he can blur the distinction between the subject and the object. Consider, for instance, his attempt to counter the tendency to turn deconstruction into a method in his famous "Letter to a Japanese friend":

> Deconstruction is not a method and cannot be transformed into one. Especially if the technical and procedural significations of the words are stressed. [...]
>
> It is not enough to say that deconstruction could not be reduced to some methodological instrumentality or a set of rules and transposable procedures. Nor will it do to claim that each deconstructive 'event' remains singular or, in any case, as close as possible to something like an idiom or a signature. It must also be made clear that deconstruction is not even an *act* or an *operation*. Not only because there would be something 'patient' or 'passive' about it (as Blanchot says, more passive than passivity, than the passivity that is opposed to activity). Not only because it does not return to an individual or a collective *subject* who would take the initiative and apply it to an object, a text, a theme, etc.
>
> Deconstruction takes place, it is an event that does not await the deliberation, consciousness, or organization of a subject, or even of modernity. *It deconstructs itself. It can be deconstructed* [*Ça se déconstruit.*] The 'it' [ça] is not here an impersonal thing that is opposed to some egological subjectivity. *It is in deconstruction* (the *Littré* says, 'to deconstruct it-self [*se déconstruire*] ... to lose its construction'). And the 'se' of 'se déconstruire', which is not the reflexivity of an ego, or of a consciousness, bears the whole enigma [...] (Derrida 1988: 3-4).

150

In some of the passages in this quotation Derrida seems to come fairly close to using formulations which Hillis Miller might have employed. Deconstruction is, for instance, described as an event that seems to be happening by itself. Yet it is obvious that Derrida in fact rules out almost everything that Hillis Miller states in the name of deconstruction. The event which Derrida is talking about is certainly not a subject-less occurrence within the text that may be detected by a reader who, in turn, performs the instrumental operation of showing how it happens. Here, the event of deconstruction becomes a riddle that cannot be solved by anyone because it is impossible to situate it precisely. The reflexive pronoun of the 'se déconstruire' is undecidable because the question of what it refers to must, by necessity, be left unanswered.

In passages like this, Derrida at least seems to border on the obscure. It is rather difficult to figure out where he leaves us with his allegedly clarifying statement. For what does it actually imply that the 'operation' of deconstruction is to be found somewhere in between activity and passivity or, perhaps, in a field of passivity that is more passive than passivity (pace the reference to Blanchot's formula)? Where does the operation actually reside if neither in an event of the text nor in an act performed by a reader? The direction of the argument is, however, clear enough. By undercutting the classical dichotomy between subject and object with the help of enigmatic formulas, Derrida obviously wants us to keep asking questions of the very kind that I just did instead of answering them with empty metaphysical formulas. Thus, what may be conceived as his 'mysticism' – as well as his extensive use of a *via negativa* by which he tries to say what cannot be stated in a straightforward language, by the way – is probably best understood as a heuristic means used for dragging us out of our habitual ways of thinking.

Because of Derrida's ability to keep his position airy or enigmatic and his unwillingness to give straightforward answers, it is often maintained that Derrida doesn't offer a theory of how texts work at all. In my view, however, this interpretation amounts to stroking the cat a little too much with the fur. It is correct that, if by a theory of the text we mean an ontological definition like the one we find in Hillis Miller, Derrida probably stays in the clear. He often explains that he is only a reader investigating the corpus of texts which controls the thought within the tradition of Western philosophy. Thus, he is only offering a hermeneutical thesis about what seems to go on in this corpus. His findings – and in particular the 'discovery' that everywhere in these texts metaphysical and counter-metaphysical motives seem to rub against each other – can only be related to the Western tradition. From the (hermeneutical) 'fact' that the texts within the Western tradition all seem to be stuck in the same kind of duality, we shouldn't – and Derrida probably doesn't – infer that all texts inevitably are. Nevertheless, it seems fair to say that Derrida's constant exposure of the aforementioned duality actually turns into something very similar to a theory of what constitutes a text in the Western tradition – a theory that is actually not so far away from the definition suggested by Hillis Miller.

In "Structure, Sign, and Play in the Discourse of the Human Sciences" Derrida, in fact, comes close to summing up his findings in an explicit definition of the Western text. Here, he draws a famous distinction between two interpretations of interpretation which seems to agree with the distinction drawn by Riddel between the modernistic nostalgia, on one hand, and the playfulness of postmodernism, on the other:

> There are thus two interpretations of interpretation, of structure, of sign, of play. The one seeks to decipher, dreams of deciphering a truth or an origin which escapes play and the order of the sign, and which lives the necessity of interpretation as an exile. The other, which is no longer turned toward the origin, affirms play and tries to pass beyond man and humanism, the name of man being the name of the being who, throughout the history of metaphysics or of onto-theology – in other words throughout the entire history – has dreamed of full presence, the reassuring foundation, the origin and the end of play (Derrida 1978: 292).

These two interpretations of interpretation are seen as the main building blocks of the texts of the metaphysical tradition. They may appear in various blends, but the point is that the two interpretations of interpretation "are absolutely irreconcilable even if we live them simultaneously and reconcile them in an obscure economy", as Derrida puts it,

> For my part, although these two interpretations must acknowledge and accentuate their difference and define their irreducibility, I do not believe that today there is any question of *choosing* – in the first place because here we are in a region [...] where the category of choice seems particularly trivial; and in the second [sic!], because we must first try to conceive of the common ground, and the difference of this irreducible *difference* (Derrida 1978: 293).

Thus, what in Hillis Miller is theorised as the heterogeneity of the text and in de Man as a discrepancy between referentiality and rhetoricity appears, in Derrida, as an obscure economy consisting of two irreconcilable, yet paradoxically interrelated interpretations of interpretation. If no choice between the two is possible, it is because, as Derrida says, we live them simultaneously. Hence, we are obliged to consider the difference of the difference between the two interpretations of interpretation.

At this point I have to raise the question about unnecessary metaphysics once again. Having pointed out the similarity between Derrida's notion of the text as an obscure economy and the notions of the text suggested by Hillis Miller and de Man, I need to consider whether Derrida is any better in avoiding the snares of metaphysics than his fellow deconstructors. Does it, in other words, make a difference to conceive the duality of the text as an obscure economy? I believe that the correct answer is yes and no. In order to see why the question deserves an ambiguous answer, we need to get somewhat closer to an understanding of what Derrida means by conceiving the difference of the irreducible difference of the two interpretations of interpretation.

Readers of Derrida will know what he is hinting at. The common ground of the difference is, of course, *la différance*. In the quotation Derrida evokes the (non)original difference which he considers the condition of possibility of all distinctions, hence also the distinction between the two interpretations of interpretations. In so far as any version of the obscure economy of the (Western) text originates in *la différance*, the simultaneous co-presence of the two irreconcilable interpretations of interpretation will always bear witness to this (non)original 'origin'. I deliberately use the phrase that I have picked up from Lyotard in order to indicate that Derrida with his idea of *la différance* as the common ground of the two interpretations of interpretation seems to place his obscure economy in the vicinity of the aesthetics of the sublime. Like the other versions of the sublime we seem to be dealing with a type of text which is bearing witness to something which is, by necessity, ineffable: In so far as the 'original' difference is nothing but the condition of possibility for manifest distinctions, it can, of course, only be hinted at.

Yet in dealing with Derrida we must be cautious not to pass judgement too hastily. Like Deleuze and Guattari, Derrida does his utmost to eradicate the link to the tradition of the sublime. Derrida's famous essay "La différance" may actually be understood as an attempt to counter the potential linkage of his thought to this tradition. At any rate Derrida tries to disentangle the inexpressibility of *la différance* from the inexpressibility at work in the classical understanding of the sublime. If *la différance* is ineffable, it is because

> one can expose only that which at a certain moment can become *present*, manifest, that which can be shown, presented as something present, a being-present in its truth, in the truth of a present or the presence of the present. Now if *différance* is X (and I also cross out the 'is X') what makes possible the presentation of the being-present, it is never presented as such. It is never offered to the present (Derrida 1982: 6).

Thus, the impossibility of stating the 'original' difference explicitly stems from the fact that it is only discernible from the traces it leaves because it never comes in the form of presence. The ultimate negativity of *la différance* makes a world of difference to Derrida. He realises that he is getting very close to creating a form of negative theology, but he insists on the importance to separate *la différance* from the concept of God governing this theology. According to Derrida, negative theology is

[...] always concerned with disengaging a supraessentiality beyond the finite categories of essence and existence, that is, of presence, and always hastening to recall that God is refused the predicate of existence, only in order to acknowledge his superior, inconceivable, and ineffable mode of being (ibid.).

If *la différance* is no less ineffable than the God of negative theology (and, for that matter, any other candidate for the position of the sublime referent), it is for opposite reasons. To Derrida, the notion of a super-being who is characterised by having a supra-essentiality must be considered an ultimate example of the metaphysics of presence to which he is opposed. In so far as God is endowed with a supra-essence, his absence becomes but a temporary substitute for an ultimate presence. By contrast, *la différance* is nothing but a void in which the only thing that is absent is – absence.

If Derrida believes that he transgresses the tradition of the sublime, even if he uses formulas that seem to recall this tradition, it is due to the particular reason for the inexpressibility of *la différance*. Having neither existence nor essence, *la différance* is incapable of becoming the sublime object of the text – simply because it isn't an object at all. If it may be argued, furthermore, that Derrida is less inclined to using unnecessary pieces of metaphysics than Hillis Miller and de Man, it is not only because he doesn't succumb to a straightforward aestheticism like Hillis Miller. It is also because it seems wrong to accuse him of construing an inversed form of metaphysics like the metaphysics of exteriority that I discerned in de Man: In so far as, in Derrida, the obscure economy of the text bears witness to nothing but the absent void of *la différance,* we do not seem to be dealing with a substitution for the metaphysical referent (like, for instance the sheer rhetoricity of language) at work.

This is, however, only one reading of what goes on in Derrida. It may also be argued (as Rorty does) that the difference that Derrida works so hard to establish doesn't make such a crucial difference after all. No matter how many pirouettes Derrida makes in order to withdraw la différance from the metaphysics of presence, the very notion of an 'original' difference may still be seen as a transcendental, or at least quasi-transcendental, concept. Derrida may have substituted the idea of an ultimate presence for an idea of an ultimate absence, but *structurally* we don't seem to have left transcendentalism. Perhaps it could be maintained that Derrida has simply taken the negativity of negative theology to its utmost consequence. Maybe he is not so much transgressing negative theology, but rather establishing a *negative* version of negative theology. Or phrased in relation to the question of the sublime: The result of the Derridean enterprise may be seen as an odd inversed version of the romanticist aesthetics of the sublime; if, in Romanticism (as presented by Schlegel, Schelling, and Novalis), "die unendliche Annäherung" is heading in the direction of absolute identity, Derrida's version of deconstruction is heading in the direction of 'absolute difference'. If Derrida's enterprise is seen in this light, it appears to be no less dependent on the aesthetics of the sublime than, say, Deleuze's and Guattari's rhizomatics – or, for that matter, de Man's programme of creating a rhetorical rhetoric. Indeed, it differs from tradition – as a matter of fact, it differs a lot – but it may still be seen as yet another version of the transcendental endeavour to capture sublimity: Bearing witness to a non-original 'origin' without being is still about naming an ineffable origin.

It is the possibility of this second view of the ultimate difference to which the obscure economy of the two interpretations of interpretation bears witness that has made me suggest that, after all, the point I made about de Man may be recycled in relation to Derrida. If we compare Derrida and de Man, it seems fair to say that la différance have taken the place which the rhetorical dimension holds in de Man. Even if we admit that Derrida succeeds in going one step further in the quest for 'the other' of metaphysics by placing a void of difference at the position held by the rhetorical dimension of language, he still seems to be caught in a negative dependence of the tradition of the sublime. Like in de Man, furthermore, it seems to be the very will to transgress the metaphysical tradition by raising a philosophy from the other side of metaphysics that obliges Derridean deconstruction to become more dependent on metaphysical thought than need be. It is, in other words, the intention to get at the 'original' difference (which cannot be named) that links Derrida closer to transcendentalism than he would like to be.

If I am not mistaken in my account of Derrida, we seem to be faced with the following alternative. We can either try to become a model reader and follow Derrida's intentions (or, to be more precise, the *intentio operis* at work in Derrida's texts) or we can look at the Derridean concept of the text as an obscure economy from the outside. Grabbing the first horn, we would have to oppose the reading that transposes *la différance* into a sublime object of the dual text. In so far as Derrida deliberately denies the non-entity any kind of being, it seems unfair to conceive it in terms of the metaphysics of presence. On this account, the only relapse into metaphysics of which Derrida is guilty is giving a name to a void that (as a non-entity) cannot be named. This 'flaw' (of which Derrida willingly admits being guilty) would have to be counted among the inevitable pieces of metaphysics, however, because the only other option than using a metaphysical name for the extra-metaphysical difference would have been silence. Regarding Derrida's enterprise from the outside leads to the view, on the other hand, that his idea of the text as an obscure economy is tied too much to the tradition of metaphysics because of the reiteration of formulas known from the aesthetics of the sublime. Even if the transcendental condition of possibility has become a difference with no existence and no essence, Derrida seems to let the Platonic (and more specifically the Kantian) tradition set the agenda.

With this conclusion about the Derridean enterprise I have come to the end of my investigation of what is offered by deconstruction. It is time for summing up. I have taken an interest in this approach to texts because, for my purposes, the concept of the text as heterogeneous seems to point in the right direction in so far as we are looking for a third way to conceive the work of art. Looking for an undialectical way to solve the double impossibility of maintaining the classical concept of the work of art, on the one hand, and transgressing it, on the other, the conception of the text as an obscure economy understood as a paradoxical combination of closure and openness indeed seems promising as a model to be generalised. Yet, the deconstructivist concept of the text may not balance so well on the margins of philosophy as it is supposed to. I have tried to show that, in Hillis Miller, the reinvestment in unnecessary metaphysical formulas is obvious. Since his version of the obscure economy turns out to be more or less an updated version of the view of the text to be found in New Criticism, it doesn't really make a difference. I have also tried to show that, going to Derrida via de Man, the relapses into an unnecessary use of metaphysics seem to become less and less obvious, but that even the version of the obscure economy presented by Derrida may be too committed to the tradition of metaphysics. If we choose to observe de Man and Derrida from the outside, it looks as if even Derrida (like de Man) is an heir of the transcendentalist aesthetics of the sublime. I have, finally, offered a possible explanation of the negative dependence. I have suggested that it is the very will to capture the absolute other of metaphysics – or, perhaps, the anxiety of falling prey to metaphysical closure or, in yet another key, the ethical drive to avoid any allegedly amoral metaphysical closure – that paradoxically threatens to lead even radical deconstruction back to metaphysics.

If this is a feasible explanation of the negative dependence on metaphysics inherent in radical deconstruction, we seem to be in need of a more 'laid-back' alternative to Derridean deconstruction. What is needed, so it seems, is a model for conceiving the work of art which is post-deconstructive in so far as it retains the best from deconstruction while avoiding to be caught in an unnecessary relapse into metaphysics. We must look for a notion of the work of art based on the following three premises: a) It must be founded on a philosophy of difference which is less concerned with getting at 'the other' of metaphysics than deconstruction; b) hence, it must rely on an alternative view of what it may mean to stay in the margins of philosophy; and

c) it must take its point of departure in the paradoxical combination of closure and openness inherent in the idea of the obscure economy, but it must complete the attempt to cut the ties to the aesthetics of the sublime. I have already announced that I find a possible solution in Luhmann. It is now time to show why.

The constructivist alternative: From obscure economy to operative closure

Initially, it should be noted that Luhmann's constructivist version of systems theory is no less based on a philosophy of difference than post-structuralism in general and deconstruction in particular – although Luhmann relies on other sources of inspiration. In Luhmann's difference-theoretical thought, the leading star is George Spencer-Brown, *not*, as in post-structuralism, Nietzsche and Heidegger (or, for that matter, Bergson). Very often Luhmann returns to Spencer-Brown's so-called calculus of form for theoretical back-up. The crucial point in this calculus is the idea that there can be no indication without a distinction. Whenever we want to indicate something, we have to draw a distinction which cleaves the space into a marked and an unmarked part. Without this distinction, no form will emerge. Thus, form is always a two-side form (distinguishing between an inside and an outside) which is based on an initial distinction, "eine Leitdifferenz" as Luhmann calls it.

I mention the difference of theoretical sources of inspiration because the choice of starting points seems to make an important difference in terms of the fundamental attitude towards difference. Even if Luhmann happily agrees with Derrida that difference 'comes first', the inspiration from Spencer-Brown gives his systems theory a more relaxed touch than the dramatic and tragic way of philosophising which, in deconstruction, comes out of taking the lead from Nietzsche and Heidegger. Whereas Derrida insists on struggling to discern an (almost) unintelligible *différance*, Luhmann simply follows the relatively cool advice given by Spencer-Brown: "Draw a distinction". This point of departure makes him become a constructivist. As far as I can see, it is the transition from a deconstructivist (Nietzsche-Heideggerian) suggestion to a constructivist (Spencer-Brownian) idea as to how we may overcome the metaphysics of presence that allows Luhmann to be more 'laid-back' than Derrida – even if his form of constructivism is, after all, less relaxed than Rorty's neo-pragmatist constructivism.

Rorty offers a very radical way of overcoming the metaphysical tradition. He takes his cue from *late* Heidegger who, after a long philosophical career with an attempt to transgress the onto-theological tradition on the agenda, suggests that we simply leave metaphysics to itself. One of Rorty's favourite quotations is from Heidegger's book *On Time and Being* in which Heidegger maintains that "a regard for metaphysics still prevails even in the intention to overcome metaphysics. Therefore our task is to cease all overcoming, and leave metaphysics to itself" (Rorty 1991: 95). In neo-pragmatism, then, the 'solution' becomes a decision to stop looking for solutions. Rorty often laments that apparently Heidegger wasn't capable of taking his own medicine. As opposed to Heidegger, however, he is more than willing to take the piece of advice. As I have already pointed out, he is ready to give up the theoretical enterprise altogether. He wants to take constructivism to its logical consequence by reorienting our intellectual powers to the task of inventing life enhancing values. Because of his decision to leave metaphysics to itself, Rorty seems to go 'beyond' cognition. Instead of thinking intellectual endeavours in terms of knowledge, he tends to stress the *strategic* dimension of the constructions he makes. For him, an operation of observation is but a re-description made in order to make something 'look good' (or at least better than something else), i.e. to dress up certain values theoretically.

I evoke Rorty's attempt to actively forget the metaphysical tradition in order to get closer to the way in which Luhmann's constructivism seems to be relaxed by specifying how it isn't. Luhmann considers himself to be as constructivist as Rorty. He has got no quarrel with Rorty about the status of a re-description (or, phrased in the language preferred by Luhmann: an operation of observation). Like Rorty, he considers operations of observation to be constructions produced by particular observers. Consequently, Luhmann also follows Rorty in admitting that constructions are contingent in so far as the distinctions on which they rely could have been drawn differently. As Luhmann wants to stay on the cognitive track, however, he cannot be satisfied with the Rortyan 'solution' to the problem of overcoming metaphysics. In so far as he is concerned about the production of some sort of understanding, he must look for a theoretical platform which can count as a foundation for post-metaphysical theory. It is for this reason that he needs the calculus of form presented by Spencer-Brown (as well as the biology of Humberto Maturana and the mathematics of Heinz von Foerster, to mention but a few of the other sources of inspiration on which Luhmann relies). With the help of this mental framework, Luhmann can replace the lax pluralism of neo-pragmatism (which he considers "the laziest of all compromises") with what, in *Observations on Modernity*, he calls a "difference-theoretical relativism" (Luhmann 1998: 27 and 29). This form of relativism is as pluralistic as neo-pragmatism in so far as it accepts several possible ways of describing the world, but it doesn't stop with the simple agreement to disagree. From the view that any operation of observation is relative to the initial distinction on which an observing system relies follows not only that the operation must be considered contingent. It also has to be admitted, on the other hand, that the particular re-description is cogent for as long as this very distinction is kept in place (provided, of course, that there are no damaging logical flaws in the argument). Thus, in a difference-theoretical relativism the various observing systems must be taken seriously as various forms of knowledge to be (re)described.

It is Luhmann's intention to stay on the cognitive track which makes me conclude that his form of constructivism is not quite as relaxed as Rorty's neo-pragmatism. Yet, by the same token, it seems to be less high-strung than Derrida's deconstruction. Even if, in opposition to Rorty, he agrees with Derrida that we need to develop a theory of difference as a post-metaphysical form of thinking, his solution to the problem of escaping metaphysics differs substantially from the deconstructivist proposal. Elsewhere (cf. Lehmann 2004), I have attempted to pin down some of the crucial differences between Derrida and Luhmann (while distinguishing both of them from Deleuze and Rorty). Here, I only need to juxtapose the two in terms of whose way of transgressing metaphysics seems to be better equipped for avoiding superfluous metaphysical leftovers. As Luhmann juxtaposes his own version of systems theory with deconstruction in the article "Deconstruction as Second-Order Observation", it seems to be a good point of departure for the comparison.

In Luhmann's juxtaposition both the closeness and the distance of Luhmannian systems theory to Derridean deconstruction become very explicit. As I have already shown, Luhmann agrees with Derrida that we need to build a theory based on difference: without an initial distinction, no system. This agreement with Derrida leads Luhmann to praise deconstruction for destroying the "one observer – one nature – one world assumption"; for illustrating that postulates of identity "have to be deconstructed"; and for showing us that observations (including one's own operations of observation), are, in principle, deconstructible (Luhmann 1993: 765). These positive remarks about deconstruction show that Luhmann counts Derrida as a brother in arms in so far as the attempt to transgress metaphysics is concerned. In spite of the positive evaluation of deconstruction, however, Luhmann is somewhat more critical towards deconstruction than the title he has chosen for the article seems to suggest. The title evokes a will to teaming up with deconstruction (in so far as deconstruction is posited *as* a form of the second-order observation that Luhmann favours), but the project launched by Luhmann rather seems to be about going 'beyond' deconstruction – about going "*from* deconstruction *to* second-order observation", to use his own words (Luhmann 1993: 769, italics added).

In fact, Luhmann passes a very Derridean judgment on Derrida. Like Derrida discerns various forms of inversed metaphysics in the theoreticians who try to overcome the tradition of metaphysics, Luhmann tends to find in deconstruction an unnecessary negative dependence on metaphysics. Having accounted for the Derridean attempt to deconstruct the assumption of presence by introducing so-called undecidable 'concepts' like *la différance*, he concludes about deconstruction:

> It is like dancing around the golden calf while knowing that an unqualifiable god has already been invented. Or, in systems terms, is deconstruction the self-organization of this dance, complaining about the lost tradition *and becoming, by this very complaint, dependent on this tradition,* [...]? (Luhmann 1993: 766, my italics).

The point Luhmann makes is fairly similar to the point I have already made about Derridean deconstruction (which is, to be honest, not only inspired by Rorty's view of deconstruction, but also Luhmann's reading as presented in "Deconstruction as Second-order Observing"), but he stages it a little differently. To Luhmann, the problem is that the quest for a difference which is inconceivable within the tradition of metaphysics becomes unnecessarily bound to the problem about being and non-being in classical ontology. In so far as it is important for Derrida to purge *la différance* of any presence, being, and essence, it still seems to be the ontological question that configures the thought. Formulated from within the systems theoretical horizon, Derrida seems to grant an unwarranted privilege to a particular distinction (being/non-being) which is, in fact, as contingent as any other distinction.

Luhmann doesn't formulate his view in so many words, but his point is evidently that Derrida is too monomaniacal in his deconstruction of the copula. The struggle against the use of the copula leads Derrida to becoming solely interested in bringing to the fore *la différance*. Because of the fight against the copula, *la différance*, as the 'origin' of all discourse, not only seems to become the 'telos' towards which all Derrida's interpretations strive; 'absolute difference' becomes the (non-)thing that Derrida heroically and constantly wrenches from the hands of the metaphysicists who use the copula naively, so to speak. It also pervades Derrida's own writing. The

163

struggle to avoid the snares of metaphysics forces Derrida to become self-deconstructive. In order to avoid being caught unnecessarily in metaphysical figures of speech he finds it necessary to let his own discourse mark an awareness of *la différance*. In his attempt to describe and at the same time avoid describing deconstruction, we have already seen the particular double writing of Derrida at work. Being committed to avoiding a straightforward copula, Derrida feels obliged to say something and, in the very same gesture, call it back by putting his own discourse under erasure. In the eyes of Luhmann, however, this very commitment to avoiding the copula links Derrida unnecessarily to ontological metaphysics.

Based on this 'insight' into the mechanics of deconstruction (or this re-description of deconstruction, as it were), Luhmann suggests another way to avoid being unnecessarily caught by the metaphysical use of the copula. He is willing to admit that "the problem lies in the copula 'is' used to formulate the question"; yet, he goes on,

> [we] can easily avoid its ontological implication (that there is only one observer) by using the second-level observation. The question then becomes: Who is to be observed and by whom and for what reason? (Luhmann 1993: 773).

This is the solution of a constructivist, not a deconstructivist. Instead of hunting down the difference that allegedly works as the (self-undermining) condition of possibility of all observing systems, Luhmann suggests that we take an interest in the observing systems that have actually been produced (by this difference) and regard them as constructions based on various distinctions. This is the point in asking 'the who-question' which shouldn't be misunderstood in any anthropomorphic sense. In Luhmann, asking who is observing simply means investigating which system works as the reference for the actual operation of observation, i.e. figuring out to which initial distinction the observation should be referred.

To Luhmann, then, the problem isn't so much the straight-forward use of the copula, but rather the fact that the metaphysicist forgets that his (observing) system is but one of many possible ways of describing the matter in sight. As soon as you move to the level of second-order observation (on which alleged first-order observations are observed in order to figure out how they are composed), this oblivion can no longer be sustained. In spite of the more or less naïve use of the copula at the level of first-order observation, it will become obvious that observations at this level are but the products of particular distinctions. The same goes, of course, for your own second-order observations of the first-order observations. That is why it is also necessary to ask *by whom* an observation of an observing system is performed. We also need, in turn, to observe our own observation in terms of the distinction on which it is based. Thus, Luhmann is as self-reflexive as Derrida, but at the level of self-reflexivity it is, once again, striking that Luhmann tackles the problem with the use of the copula very differently from Derrida. Instead of insisting, like Derrida, on a double discourse which constantly undermines itself, Luhmann prefers to solve the problem by doing one operation of observation at a time. Instead of writing under erasure, Luhmann places his writing under erasure from the outset, so to speak, by admitting that it should only be considered a construction based on a particular (contingent) distinction. Instead of undermining himself constantly, he can talk as if he was presenting a straight-forward, almost positivistic, theory – in the hope that his audience will keep in mind that it is a construction itself which is, in principle, deconstructible.

In short, Luhmann bets on accepting a plurality of observing systems as the privileged means to overcome the ontological presumptions of metaphysics. Instead of always, like Derrida, evoking the fundamental and extra-metaphysical difference behind these systems, he is satisfied with dissolving "the one observer – one nature – one world assumption" by showing that there are always several observers. To me, it makes sense to see this pluralistic 'solution' inherent in Luhmann's difference-theoretical relativism as an approach which is struggling with deconstruction to obtain the position in the margins of philosophy, but without becoming too concerned about 'the other' of metaphysics.

With his difference-theoretical relativism, Luhmann indeed seems to transgress metaphysics. In a world consisting of many, competing observing systems there is no room for ontology as there can be no privileged distinction holding the key to reality. Thus, Luhmann is no longer inside the closure of metaphysics. Nor is he, however, completely outside. It is difficult to deny that, with his use of a seemingly referential language, Luhmann re-uses the vocabulary of metaphysics. In so far as (by 'solving' the problem with the inherent ontology in the copula with invisible quotation marks posited from the outset) he can regain a straight-forward kind of writing, he has only transformed the one ontology of the metaphysical tradition into as many 'as if'-ontologies as there are observing systems. In the eyes of Luhmann, however, this constructivist way to position thought in the margins of philosophy seems better equipped to avoid unnecessary relapses into metaphysics than deconstruction because it doesn't let the agenda be decided by ontological questions. As we have seen, Luhmann tends to see Derrida's struggle to pin down the difference that escapes metaphysics as unnecessarily committed to the ontological distinction of being and non-being. Even if *la différance* is voided of presence, the very attempt to think 'the other' of metaphysics still pertains to the distinction of classical ontology. Luhmann's suggestion seems to be: Give up this quest, think difference in terms of a plurality of distinctions instead – and this problem will at least dissolve!

In so far as this suggestion will actually diminish the problem about the return of unnecessarily metaphysical mental habits, i.e. if Luhmann's constructivist version of a difference-theoretical 'solution' to the problem is better than the deconstructivist, I may hope to find a concept of the work of art in systems theory which is more suitable for my purposes. Before I move on to the issue of aesthetics, however, I would like to consider the claim that Luhmann's solution is better than Derrida's.

If, for a moment, I suspend the (second-order) operation of observation which I am offering here in order to view it from the outside (i.e. at the level of third-order observation), it will become obvious that my account of Derrida's deconstruction is made on the basis of the initial distinction of systems theory. As we have seen, the complaint about the negative dependence on metaphysics only appears feasible in one out of two possible readings of Derrida. A Derridean, subscribing to the other reading of Derrida, would undoubtedly tend to inverse the judgment. From a deconstructivist point of view, the Luhmannian constructivism would appear as being as much pervaded by superfluous metaphysics as Derridean deconstruction appears to be in the perspective of systems theory. In so far as you believe that the copula has got to be opposed with any means available, a straightforward description of observing systems is bound to look like sheer metaphysics. How does an initial admittance of the fact that we are only dealing with a construction change anything if it doesn't really alter our approach to descriptions? Doesn't this strategy actually amount to a simple re-introduction of the classical relation between subject and object? And so on and so forth.

On difference-theoretical grounds there is no way to settle this dispute. Formulated in Luhmannian terms, the question about which of the views you favour is a matter of which initial distinction you draw. Depending on the distinction "constructivist systems theory / deconstruction" means siding with Luhmann. By contrast, you would tend to side with Derrida if you rely on the distinction "deconstruction / constructivist systems theory" – which must be considered a very different distinction because of the inversion of self-reference and exterior reference. At this third-order level of observation, thus, it not only becomes visible that my (re)description of deconstruction as being unnecessarily related to the tradition of metaphysics is Luhmannian (as it relies on a distinction produced from within systems theory). It also becomes obvious that this (re)description is no more valid than a possible deconstructive (re)description of systems theory would be.

If I am to finish my enterprise, however, I see no other solution than taking the piece of advice offered by Luhmann about doing one operation of observation at a time and go on with my Luhmannian re-description of the situation. Seen from this perspective, Derrida's quest for 'the other' of metaphysics still tends to look a little too much like an unnecessary way to play the good old metaphysical game of outdoing all former theoreticians by naming the very principle that they were incapable of grasping. Thus, continuing my line of thinking based on a preference of Luhmann's way to operate in the margins of philosophy, I shall now ask whether Luhmann has got a better model to offer regarding the work of art than the model offered by deconstruction. More specifically the question becomes: Does, in fact, a model which may be seen as an improvement of the obscure economy because it escapes the aesthetics of the sublime spring from the difference-theoretical relativism of Luhmann? I think that it does, as will appear.

It should be noted, though, that Luhmann isn't particularly interested in the question of the *singular* work of art. *Die Kunst der Gesellschaft* is by and large an investigation of why we have got a subsystem in our society called art and what constitutes it. In this *sociological* context, the investigation cannot be about "observing works of art" and, by consequence, Luhmann must warn us in the preface that "in so far as art is concerned, we are not offering a helpful theory" (Luhmann 2000: 3, translation modified). There is some truth to this laconic self-evaluation, but it nevertheless seems to be a little too harsh. Even if it isn't his key concern to do so, Luhmann actually offers a model for conceiving the work of art which is, for my purposes at least, very helpful. Indeed, it doesn't spring from a great amount of analyses of works of art from which he may inductively extrapolate a concept of the work of art. As a matter of fact, not even a single analysis of a work of art can be found in his book. Luhmann's strategy is more deductive. Thus, the model for conceiving the work of art is rather raised with the help of the notions which carries his overall systems theory.

As all other observing systems, a work of art is seen as a two-side form based on an initial distinction producing an asymmetrical relation between self-reference and exterior reference. This distinction allows for the addition of further (two-side) forms – *but only on the inside of the initial distinction*. This view is explicitly opposed to the mimetic tradition according to which a work of art is first and foremost understood as a representation of life. It goes without saying that, on the constructivist grounds on which Luhmann operates, the forms produced by the work of art cannot be conceived as a mirror that 'comes after' reality. Instead they must be seen as the products of a self-organising system which produces by itself the differences it uses. In so far as an image of reality results from this operation, it should only be considered an *effect* of the differences employed by the work of art. Grafting the logics of Spencer-Brown onto the constructivist biology of Maturana, Luhmann looks for an approach that is "compatible with the idea of autopoiesis" which guides his overall notion of communication, i.e. an approach which "assumes that the operative closure of autopoietic systems produces a *difference*, namely, the difference between system and environment" (Luhmann 2000: 13).

The work of art as an autopoietic, i.e. self-producing and self-reproducing, system – can I seriously mean that? And does Luhmann actually mean that? How can it make sense to talk about a work of art as if it can be produced by itself? If we are going to use the term autopoiesis at all in relation to art in a meaningful way, wouldn't it at least be reasonable to restrict ourselves to using it for describing the particular works of art that are in fact created 'on the spot', so to speak. I am thinking of event-like works of art which only come into being when received, i.e. works of the type that Eco has called, in "The Poetics of the Open Work", *works-in-movement* (cf. Eco 1981: 56). Shouldn't we, in other words, make use of the distinction between *allo-* and *auto*poietic systems that Bo Kampmann Walther has lifted out of Luhmann in order to determine the difference between the computer and the human mind (cf. Walter 2002: 302). If allopoietic systems (like, for instance, a computer) are defined as being *extrinsically* determined, it seems reasonable to consider an 'ordinary' work of art to be such a system. It is, after all, a product created by an artist. Considering an event-like work of art which is created only during the process of reception, by contrast, the idea of autopoiesis (suggesting a system which is only *intrinsically* determined like, for instance, the human mind) seems to be somewhat more adequate. A work-in-movement seems at least to be self-inaugurating in the sense that it isn't finished until the recipient intervenes. Interactive multimedia installations come to mind – or perhaps performative forms of art more generally.

This somewhat more obvious way of employing the idea of autopoiesis may, in fact, be found in the attempt by Fischer-Lichte to determine the particularity of performative art that I have mentioned earlier. For this purpose the notion of autopoiesis comes in handy – even if she seems to be a little uncertain about how she wants to draw the distinction between autopoietic and non-autopoietic forms of art.

At times, she tends to use the idea of autopoiesis in order to define performative art as such. Drawing a distinction between performative art and all other art forms, she insists on "die leibliche Ko-Präsenz von Akteuren und Zuschauern" as the constituting trait of the performative (Fischer-Lichte 2004: 47). Because of this bodily co-presence of the actors *as well as* the spectators in performative art, the recipients become "im emphatischen Sinne zu 'Schöpfern' der Aufführung" (Fischer-Lichte 2004: 48). In so far as the rules of the production are "prinzipiel verhandelbar", they are "einerseits von den Schauspielern (und dem Regisseur), andererseits von den Zuschauern aufgestellt worden" (ibid.). Thus, it is the unfinished character of a performance due to its openness to negotiations between the artists and the spectators during the actual running time that makes Fischer-Lichte determine performative art as autopoietic.

At other times, however, she draws a slightly different distinction. When defending an idea of a performative turn within the art world in the sixties, the distinction is transformed into a difference between the strategies of the avant-garde and the strategies employed by 'ordinary' art in general and the classical theatre in particular:

Mit der performativen Wende in den sechziger Jahren ging eine neue Haltung gegenüber der Kontingenz einher. Sie wurde nun überwiegend als Bedingung der Möglichkeit von Aufführungen nicht nur akzeptiert, sondern ausdrücklich begrüsst. Das Interesse richtete sich nun explizit auf die *feedback*-Schleife als selbstbezügliches, autopoietisches System mit prinzipiell offenem, nicht vorhersagbarem Ausgang, das sich durch Inszenierungsstrategien weder tatsächlich unterbrechen noch gezielt steuern lässt. Dabei verschob sich das Interesse von einer möglichen Kontrolle des Systems zu seinem besonderen Modus der Autopoiesis (Fischer-Lichte 2004: 61).

Here, the notion of autopoiesis becomes linked to the celebration of contingency, uncontrollability, and open-endedness which characterises the avant-garde. In this strain of the text, Fischer-Lichte only seems to be willing to characterise a (historically emergent) part of performative art as autopoietic – and, by the same token, relegate a great deal of theatre and other 'normal' performative forms of art to the outside of the distinction between autopoietic and non-autopoietic art.

In spite of the equivocation concerning where to draw the line, however, the idea that we need to make such a distinction is constant. Whether she determines performative art as such or only the avant-garde version of performative art as autopoietic, the crucial point is that Fischer-Lichte wants to reserve the term to works of art that live by the "feedback-Schleife" between co-present and hence co-creative producers and recipients.

I evoke the view offered by Fischer-Lichte in order to clarify Luhmann's position by presenting a road *not* taken by Luhmann – or, at any rate, a road which I *believe* that Luhmann neither takes nor can take. The question of which systems should be considered autopoietic takes us to the heart of Luhmann's system theory and his position regarding this problem is not always evident. By consequence, I shall have to admit that I continue my argument with a certain amount of concern: Have I misunderstood Luhmann on this crucial point? However, the show must go on. Therefore, I shall try to substantiate the view that Luhmann actually thinks of the work of art as such as an autopoietic system as convincingly as possible.

It is, indeed, possible to use the concept of autopoiesis to establish a distinction between different forms of art, but if I read Luhmann correctly, this use of the notion would be like barking up the wrong tree. To him, forms of art that are based on a co-presence of producer and recipient do not represent a difference of *kind*. As a matter of fact, he seems to agree with the theoreticians presented in the beginning of this article who see the work of art as being, *in principle,* determined by temporality as well as by the recipient's 'complicity' in the production of meaning. It is important to remember that "communication through art, too, must take time into account", Luhmann says and explains how this should be understood:

> The point is not only that the artist must produce the work before it can be perceived. Any observing participation is, on the contrary, a temporal process, a systematically ordered succession of events. Not only the actions of production must succeed one another in time and orient themselves recursively in relation to what has already been decided and to possibilities opened or eliminated by these decisions. Also the perception gains access to the work of art in temporal terms, i.e. by actualising step by step the references in the context of distinctions that shift from moment to moment (Luhmann 2000: 20-1, translation modified).

Iser couldn't have put it any better. The work of art is considered temporal in so far as it is only actualised in the process of reception. Even if the producer of a classical work of art has left us with what seems to be an atemporal product, the work of art is, in fact, still in flux because the context of the involved distinctions shifts in the process of reception. Consequently, an 'ordinary' work of art only appears to be allopoietic, i.e. controlled in advance by an external producer. In fact, it is no less constituted in the flux of reception than works-in-movement. Even if it appears to be a fixed and pre-produced entity, its meaning is constantly transformed by the actualisations of the various readers.

Luhmann is aware of the need to draw a distinction between performative and other forms of art evoked by Fischer-Lichte, to be sure, but he tends to see it only as a difference of *degree.* Having presented his observations of the temporality of art, Luhmann continues:

> These observations *apply to art in general,* not only to the obvious cases of music, dance, or stage productions, in which the artwork exists only as a pure

sequence of events. On the contrary, such forms of art present a special case in which a synchronised sequence of performance and experience makes possible an often described heightened sense of simultaneity (Luhmann 2000: 21, translation modified, italics added).

Here, Luhmann willingly admits that performative works of art represent a special case, but only in so far as they produce a heightened sense of simultaneity, *not* in the sense that, by this very trait, they become more temporal, more open-ended, or more autopoietic than 'ordinary' works of art. As there are no forms of art which are able to withdraw from temporality, it doesn't seem to make sense to draw a distinction between allo- and autopoietic works of art.

However, the real difficulty in trying to extrapolate a concept of the work of art from Luhmann may be that, at times, he talks as if he is unwilling to think of the work of art as a system at all. As I have pointed out earlier, he is first and foremost interested in (re-)describing the communication system art as such. In this attempt the singular works of art tend to be reduced to the recursive manoeuvres which this particular social subsystem must use for the sake of reproduction, i.e. to *components* within a larger autopoietic and operatively closed system. In so far as Luhmann thinks of these components as bits and pieces of communication (and how could he think of them otherwise if he determines a social system as nothing but communication), however, it seems inevitable to think of them as systems of the very same kind as the social system itself. Any communication about art is an operation of observation based on a particular distinction and in so far as the work of art is considered as much a part of the communication as any other form of communicative operation, it also seems cogent to see it as an observing system.

Perhaps it could be argued that we are dealing with two different forms of observing systems and that only the social system at large should be considered an autopoietic system whereas the systems working as the components of this autopoietic system should not. I think, however, that this solution would work against the general direction of Luhmann's argument. Again, it is interesting to compare

173

Luhmann with Fischer-Lichte. She picks up the notion of autopoiesis from Maturana. This gives her thought a certain *biologistic* touch. If she finds it reasonable to draw a distinction between auto- and allopoietic forms of art, it seems to be due to the fact that her argument is carried by an implicit distinction between the living process (of performative or avant-garde art) and the dead object (of non-performative or classical art). This distinction isn't made explicit; it is simply taken for granted. It is, however, implied in her insistence on the *bodily* co-presence of actors and spectators which is hardly fortuitous. The flesh and blood of the participants in the performative event suggests that, as opposed to other art forms, only performative art is truly alive. Indeed, Luhmann also refers to Maturana, but he generalises the idea of autopoietic systems beyond the biologism of Maturana and in this context a distinction between living and dead systems doesn't seem pertinent. Instead Luhmann must, so it seems, be led to turn any observing system into an autopoietic system.

Against this conclusion could be argued that Luhmann, also at this point, seems to waver a little. In "Deconstruction as Second-Order Observing", for instance, he seems to be saying two things at the same time. At one place he tends to establish a difference between 'ordinary' and autopoietic observing systems:

> In other words, any observing system whatever its material reality [...], can be described as determined by the distinction it uses. In the *case* of *autopoietic* (that is self-reproducing) systems, this would mean that an observer has to focus on the self-determined and self-determining distinctions a system uses to frame its own observations (Luhmann 1993: 767, first italics added).

In so far as Luhmann presents the autopoietic system as a particular case, he must fathom a form of observing systems which is not autopoietic, but later in the article he seems to rule against this possibility, after all:

> We have to define the concept of observation abstractly so that it can be applied to psychic and to social operations, to perception and thinking and

to communication as well. *Observation is nothing but making a distinction to indicate one side and not the other,* regardless of the material basis of the operation which does the job, and regardless of the boundaries that close a system (brain, mind, social system), *so that it becomes an autopoietic system* reproduced by a network of its own operations, and eventually irritated but never determined by its environment (Luhmann 1993: 773-74, my italics).

In this generalised understanding of observation the distinction between autopoietic and non-autopoietic observing systems seems to disappear. In so far as an observing system becomes an autopoietic system by the very act of observing defined abstractly as the act of drawing a distinction between self-reference and external reference, it is hard to see that there can be any non-autopoietic observing systems. And Luhmann seems to be forced to argue like this. In a constructivist framework it is inevitable to make the autopoiesis of an observing system dependent on the act of drawing a distinction since there can be no operation of observation without a self-drawn distinction. Thus, Luhmann doesn't really seem to be capable of meaning what he says in the first of the two quotations. In the generalised use of the term autopoiesis, it seems inevitable that it must embrace all observing systems – hence also, for instance, a work of art.

This is why I believe that Luhmann offers us a concept of the work of art based on the notion of the autopoietic, operatively closed observing system. At any rate, it is this very model for conceiving the work of art which I believe may serve as an alternative third way. The suggestion of an *operatively* closed system presents an alternative to the classical (metaphysical) idea of the closed work of art. It suggests a closure which is also open. But it also gives us an alternative to the avant-gardist (anti-metaphysical) concept of the open work of art as it maintains that openness always relies on some kind of closure. Like Luhmann's entire constructivist thinking seems to differ from Derridean deconstruction, furthermore, it actually also seems to represent an alternative to the obscure economy suggested by Derrida – even if it comes very close to this very idea.

If the notion of operative closure may look like an obscure economy, it is because it holds the same duplicity of closure and openness. It is turned towards closure because it is based on a distinction that secures the autopoiesis. By the same token, on the other hand, it leaves an open flank. Luhmann explains:

> An arrangement of forms creates an open flank. Despite its closure, a work of art can be observed adequately only in relation to time [...]. Thinking of the work as an arrested movement to be supplemented imaginatively by the observer does not suffice. Rather, the work's built-in temporality must be experienced as a reconstruction of *its incompletion* (Luhmann 2000: 30, italics added, translation modified).

Derrida would, no doubt, have formulated the point somewhat differently, but he would have used words to the same effect. Like in Derrida, the openness is seen as a product of the temporality involved in the work of difference that leaves the work incomplete – or, to phrase the point in Derridean terms, that turns one side of the work towards dissemination. As in Derrida, furthermore, we are dealing with a *simultaneity* in the production of closure and openness. In Luhmann, it is the very gesture of drawing a distinction that closes off the work from its environment *and* opens it to what in Luhmann is called "*Eigenkomplexität*". In spite of this similarity to the paradoxical combination of closure and openness inherent in the notion of the obscure economy, I nevertheless believe that we ought to be careful not to confuse the concept of an operatively closed work of art with this notion.

One way of phrasing the difference would be to say that the notion of an operative closure is an inversion of the obscure economy – an inversion which is completely in line with the difference between the Derridean deconstructive enterprise and the Luhmannian constructivism that I have outlined earlier. The two concepts seem to display two opposed forms of asymmetry. The obscure economy is a concept which is basically supposed to represent the idea that an alleged closure is in fact undermined by an inherent tendency to self-destruction; it is, so to speak, pointing in the direction of openness. As opposed to this, the notion of an operatively closed system is turned more towards closure; it is used by Luhmann in order to suggest that, in spite of the fact that any closure is contingent, we are still dealing with a form of closure. If I prefer the Luhmannian version of the asymmetry, it is due to the fact that it doesn't seem to be related to the aesthetics of the sublime – not even, like the concept of the obscure economy, negatively – and therefore less dependent on the tradition of metaphysics.

Luhmann does, indeed, employ formulas which seem to evoke the notion of inexpressibility. He often underlines the fact that the act of drawing a distinction renders the environment of the system invisible. In so far as the environment is only visible in the form of the system's own exterior reference, the environment itself remains a part of the unmarked space. Equally often, he stresses the fact that the *unity* of the distinction of a particular system cannot be seen by the system itself because it would demand another operation of observation, i.e. another operatively closed observing system, to point out the initial distinction of this system. Nevertheless, I find it erroneous to interpret these formulas in terms of the aesthetics of the sublime. We are not dealing with an inexpressible supra-essence to which the operatively closed work of art bears witness – let alone an ineffable supra-absence of such a supra-essence, to evoke the inversed version of the sublime which may be discerned in Derrida. Luhmann makes a much more prosaic point. In Luhmannian systems theory, the invisibility doesn't pertain to something (or the very absence of this something) which is *always* and *in principle* inexpressible. The blindnesses produced by a system are only temporary. What cannot be seen by a particular observing system may become visible if it is viewed from the perspective of other observing systems – based on other blind spots which may, in turn, be rendered visible if viewed from the outside. And so on and so forth. As this kind of ineffability doesn't suggest that there is something (or 'something') which, per definition, cannot be seen, it doesn't seem to be unnecessarily linked to the metaphysical tradition of the sublime.

Instead of sublimity, Luhmann seems to offer us a very secular idea of the work of art. Like other observing systems, a work of art simply becomes a transitory combination of elements organised around an initial distinction. For this notion of the work of art the term *network* seems to be appropriate. Luhmann, for one, has realised this. In one of the passages that I have quoted, we have already seen him talk about a network in an account of the autopoietic system and this quotation is just one example among many. In *Die Kunst der Gesellschaft,* for instance, he often uses the term when determining an operatively closed system in general and a work of art in particular. An autopoietic system can only obtain "a dynamic stability", he says, because "the elements of the system are produced and reproduced *within the network of the system's elements,* that is, through recursions" (Luhmann 2000, p. 49, translation modified, italics added). Here, Luhmann points out the three central traits of the operatively closed work of art which, to my mind, makes it feasible to think of it in terms of a network. 1) Luhmann seems to be on a par with Deleuze and Guattari who stresses the technical dimension of the rhizome by talking about an assemblage. In so far as an operatively closed system is nothing but a combination of elements, it, too, should be seen as some kind of machine. 2) An operatively closed work of art has to be seen as a self-engulfing system. The elements do not obtain the meaning from any exterior referent, but only from within the network formed by the interior elements. 3) In so far as the connection of elements can only be transitory and the stability it produces only dynamic, the operatively closed work of art is as thrown upon a temporal fragility as any other network. To my mind, this secular notion of the work of art may count as post-deconstructive.

References

Bürger, P. (1974). *Die Theorie der Avantgarde*. Frankfurt a. M.: Suhrkamp.

De Man, P. (1986). The Resistance to Theory. In *The Resistance to Theory*. Minneapolis: University of Minnesota Press.

Deleuze, G. and Guattari, F. (1976). *Rhizome. Introduction*. Paris: Les Éditions de Minuit.

Deleuze, G. and Guattari, F. (1987). Rhizome: an Introduction. In *A Thousand Plateaus*. Minneapolis: University of Minnesota.

Derrida, J. (1978). Structure, Sign, and Play in the Discourse of the Human Sciences. In *Writing and Difference*. Chicago: The University of Chicago Press.

Derrida, J. (1982). La difference. In *Margins of philosophy*. Chicago: The University of Chicago Press.

Derrida, J. (1988). Letter to a Japanese friend. In D. Wood and R. Bernasconi (eds.), *Derrida and difference*. Evanston: Northwestern University Press.

Eco, U. (1981). The Poetics of the Open Work. In *The Role of the Reader. Explorations in the Semiotics of Texts*. London: Hutchinson.

Eco, U. (1988). Intentio Lectoris: The State of the Art. In *Differentia*, nr. 2.

Eco, U. (1992a). Overinterpreting Texts. In S. Collini (ed.), *Interpretation and Overinterpretation*. Cambridge: Cambridge University Press.

Eco, U. (1992b). Between Author and Text. In S. Collini (ed.), *Interpretation and Overinterpretation*. Cambridge: Cambridge University Press.

Fish, S. (1980). *Is there a Text in this Classroom? The Authority of Interpretive Communities*. Cambridge, Mass. And London: Harvard University Press.

Fischer-Lichte, E. (2004). *Ästhetik des Performativen*. Frankfurt a.M.: Suhrkamp.

Fjord Jensen, J. (1987). Enheden af modsætninger. In *Det tredje. Den postmoderne udfordring*. Valby: Amadeus Forlag

Frank, M. (1997). *'Unendliche Annäherung'. Die Anfänge der philosophischen Frühromantik*. Frankfurt a.M.: Suhrkamp.

Hardt, M. (1993). *Gilles Deleuze. An Apprenticeship in Philosophy*. London: UCL Press.

Iser, W. (1971). Indeterminacy and the Reader's Response in Prose Fiction. In J. Hillis Miller (ed.), *Aspects of Narrative. Selected Papers from the English Institute*. New York: Columbia University Press.

Iser, W. (1988). Die Appellstruktur der Texte. In R. Warning, (ed.), *Rezeptionsästhetik*. München: Wilhelm Fink Verlag.

Jalving, C. (2005). *Værk som handling. Performativitet som kunsthistorisk metode og tema i samtidskunsten*. Ph.d.-afhandling, Københavns universitet.

Lehmann, N. (1996). *Dekonstruktion og dramaturgi*. Århus: Aarhus Universitetsforlag.

Lehmann, N. (2004). On Different Uses of Difference. Derrida, Deleuze, Luhmann, and Rorty. In *Cybernetics and Human Knowing*, vol. 11, No 3.

Luhmann, N. (1993). Deconstruction as Second-Order Observation. In *New Literary History*, no. 24.

Luhmann, N. (1997). *Die Kunst der Gesellschaft*. Frankfurt a.M.: Suhrkamp.

Luhmann, N. (1998). *Observations on Modernity*. Stanford: Stanford University Press.

Luhmann, N. (2000). *Art as a Social System*. Stanford: Stanford University Press.

Lyotard, J.-F. (1991). The Sublime and the Avant-Garde. In A. Benjamin (ed.), *The Lyotard Reader*. Oxford: Basil Blackwell.

Miller, J.H. (1975). Deconstructing the Deconstructors. *Diacritics,* summer-issue.

Miller, J.H. (1980). Theory and Practice. In *Critical Inquiry,* nr. 6.

Rorty, R. (1989). From Ironist Theory to Private Allusions: Derrida. In *Contingency, Irony, and Solidarity*. Cambridge: Cambridge University Press.

Rorty, R. (1991). Deconstruction and Circumvention. In *Essays on Heidegger and Others. Philosophical papers volume 2*. Cambridge: Cambridge University Press.

Rorty, R. (1992). The Pragmatist's Progress. In S. Collini (ed.), *Interpretation and Overinterpretation.* Cambridge: Cambridge University Press.

Walther, B.K. (2002). The Ontology of Virtual Space: In Search of Matrixes and Cube-machines. In L. Qvortrup (ed.), *Virtual Space: Spatiality in Virtual Inhabited 3D Worlds.* London: Springer-Verlag.

What Does It Imply to Operate on the Basis of Difference instead of Identity? Towards a Post-ontological Theory of Society[1]

The intellective space of difference

Dealing with a plurality of difference theories, with post-ontological ways of theorising and performative 'différance'-thinking can lead very easily to confusion. That is why it is necessary to define and cir-

---

1   As a preliminary remark I would like to precise the "genre" of my contribution. It is not meant to substantiate results by showing how the emerge from study, synthesis and advancement of existing research. The paths I am treading are somewhat solitary. This is due to the lack of an interdisciplinary effort and a correlative community of researchers dealing with the teoretical, epistemolocal and philosophical implimations of major changes in the theory building in the human and social sciences. if my concepts and my terminology seem to be in a way idiosyncratic, this is because I had no other choice than to go ahead with my reflections without waiting for the emergence of such an effort and the constitution of its conceptual space. I shall consequently limit myself in the apparatus of my present contribution to very few reference. I suppose the bulk of luhmannian system theory and cultural sciences studies as known. I do not take pains to refer to the extensive litterature existing in those fields. I shall however indicate, when indispensable, preceding works of mine on ground wich I am building here my new conceptualisations.

cumscribe one's own point of observation regarding these avenues of thought. Preliminary questions have to be put: is such an observation a descriptive one, attempting to devise entries into a new practice of thinking which is not intuitive, going against the spontaneous impulses of world perception and ordering, deconstructing whole aspects of world-givenness and opening perspectives which rather blur the sight than clarify it? Is such an observation immanent to one or the other of these new modes of thought and does it try, from its own point of observation, to gain a view of all others? While doing this, would it be possible to exclude an effect of structural inadequacy – between the elusive points of observation, which are constituted by difference theories? Would such an exploration of the intellective space in which such theories are assembled be merely classificatory in the sense that, using descriptions which I have characterised as immanent, it would construct, identify, compare and classify various figures of thought having in common their rupture with the traditional categories of the ontology, that is with identity, stability, unity, firmness of the observed under changing modes of observation? This would presuppose the possibility of an encompassing space in which such theories become commensurable, comparable and classifiable.

It is important to articulate precisely the difficulty, which is encountered in such an approach. I would formulate it in the following way: De-ontologising figures of thought is in itself "unthinkable". We should not cultivate any illusion regarding our capacities to think along de-ontologised lines of thought. In the process of such thinking we are, in fact, always re-ontologising most of the terms concerned. This I have shown in an extensive work on the epistemology of the social and human sciences[2], concentrating in its first part on Simmel and Saussure[3]. Working along the lines of the relationism of Simmel and the differentialism of Saussure I tried to give an account of the

---

2   *Sciences du sens. Perspectives théoriques,* Strasbourg Presses Universitaires de Strasbourg 2006.
3   At stake are basically Simmel's *Philosophie des Geldes* and Saussure's *Cours de linguistique générale.*

intellection processes involved in the thinking of the "absolute relation" of the former and the purely differential entity of the latter. The relapsing effect from relationist and differential projections of thought to intuitive ones showing intrinsic solidarities with the extensitivity and transitivity of usual thought schemes is structural. It is a quite painful undertaking to analyse the thought procedures enabling us to think difference in its self-elusivity as the mode of givenness of any world entity. Such an analysis shows how restricted the access to such forms of thinking is and how elusive they themselves are. There are only critical moments in such a thinking in which difference orientation can be practised on a specific segment of thought, beyond which it cannot be maintained in its full potencies.

A second difficulty is related to the fact that the space of post-ontological thought is a very chaotic one. Theoretical propositions are numerous and highly heterogeneous, ranging from Derrida to Luhmann, via Rorty and Deleuze[4]. The question is then: does it make sense to bring light, order, clarity, analyticity into this space? Since any difference in this space engulfs itself and all others in a manner that makes impossible any disentanglement and any reordering of such differences, is the thrust towards a differentiation of difference theories and their ordering, i.e. the thrust towards understanding, comprehension, intelligibility a post-ontologically justifiable one?[5]

My answer would be: yes, for two reasons: first, because the figures of classical paradox, i.e. the standard figures of self-entanglement, self-contradiction, regression to the infinite etc. are not effective in the space of post-ontological thought itself, which then is not challenged nor impugned by such figures; second, because post-ontological theory is a process of events (of differentiation) taking place as events of intellection, lighting an emergence of difference which makes a difference (that is: which matters) and has thereby an effect on the interests of those handling such an difference intellectually.

---

4   See the contribution of Niels Lehmann in *Cybernetics & Human Knowing*, vol. 11, no. 3, 2004.

5   This is Lehmann's endeavour in the above quoted contribution.

Going straight to my central thesis, I would say that the central concept of any post-ontological theory will have to be that of intellection[6].

My intention in this paper is to present a possible introduction of such a concept into the space of thought the entries of which I am trying to delineate here. My claim is that the concept of intellection is the only one enabling us to maintain a substantial negotiability between the principial unthinkability of post-ontological thought and its actual, evential continuation.

The social correlation of difference

My argument has at this juncture to introduce a term, which has not yet been evoked. My preliminary presentation did the economy of the term unintentionally, but in hindsight, quite significantly. It seems in effect possible to speak of post-ontological theories, ways of observation and ways of world perception and experience without referring to this term, namely society. Such an apparent superfluity is a crucial delusion. One would be inclined to think that society is a legitimate term that should be taken into consideration whenever theories are at stake which thematise society, communication, the individual, etc. Broadly speaking, whenever we are considering theories belonging to the social and human sciences. Society, the social in general, would represent object matters of a disciplined theoretical observation. Where they are not explicitly observed, they would have no relevance.

One has to stress very strongly the fact that society is a term implied pervasively by any difference orientation and that it is structurally immanent to any post-ontological setting. The working of difference within any field of observation is equivalent to that of a thorough contingentiation of all settings and the therein posited terms and entities. Fixed necessities maintain entities in their identity-based

6   On the meaning and structure of post-ontological theory, see the last study ("Was ist noch Theorie?") of my Kontingenz, Paradox, Nur-Vollzug. Grundprobleme einer Theorie der Gesellschaft, Konstanz UVK (Universitätsverlag Konstanz) 2004.

mould, within intrinsically determined firm limits, and they enhance continuous unequivocal identifications and re-identifications. When observation is oriented towards necessity, construct it, instruct it systematically into world sequences, then contingency is maintained at bay, and difference cannot make its irruption into the space of observation. Difference orientation is always linked to the introduction in theoretical (and practical) observation of points of view, which have contingentiating effects on the observed and the observer.

Ultimately it is the introduction, in Western culture and science, of functionalist modes of observation, which began to shake off the domination of substantialist ones. They led to nominalist modes of thought, de-realising a great number of mundane and intelligible entities[7]. From this position onward, it was the system concept, which filled more consistently and efficiently the place of the function concept and set the stage for a potentialised de-substantialisation of theory and practice. A marked transition was that accomplished by Niklas Luhmann from functionalism to what I term "equifunctionalism", designating a sort of and potentialised functionalism breaking with the last vestiges of identitarian, ontological settings within theoretical observations[8]. It led to the ripening of a sort of perfect form of post-ontological theory articulated around the concept of systemic autopoiesis.

Pervasive contingentiation of the whole of theoretical observation, that means of all areas of scientific inquiry, has been obtained through the breaking of the divide between subject and object. This has been achieved with the introduction of the idea of observation by which the object reveals itself to be the observer himself with the whole den-

---

7   Classical works reconstructing this evolution are: Rombach, Heinrich: *Substanz, System, Struktur*, Freiburg Alber 1965, and Cassirer, Ernst: *Substanzbegriff und Funktionsbegriff*, Darmstadt, Wissenschaftliche Buchgesellschaft 1976

8   The "equifunctionalism" of Luhmann is a major avenue of de-ontologisation. It has been quite neglected in comparison with the concept of autopoiesis. The whole Luhmannian critique of ontological categories of thought within the sciences of the social takes its cue from a thorough destruction of the concept of goal *(Zweck)* which is the key concept giving human action unity and transitivity. See Luhmann, Niklas: *Zweckbegriff und Systemrationalität*, Frankfurt, Suhrkamp 1973.

sity of its constructive biases. The observer on his part ceased to be thought of as a subject and has been understood as the observation itself being a texture of social processes of communication in which the observed as well as the observer came to constitution – or condensation, to use a term from Spencer Brown's *Laws of form*. This is the place at which the term society enters the space of difference and difference orientation: every observation, be it that of social interaction or of mathematical equations, is effectuated within social communication processes and what is observed in it is nothing else than the striation of the space in which the object is projected by these processes themselves.

This is the way we have to conceive the link between theory and society. Both terms, theory and society, are infinite denominators of any term which is put above them, which means that they accomplish a self- and alien-engulfing of any term put in relation to them. The more so when they themselves are put into relation to each other. I propose now to turn to the problematics of such a setting into relation of theory and society in order to explore the potential of differentiation, contingentiation, de-ontologisation and intellection born by such a relationship.

Theory and society

There seems to be a problem with a science of society under the post-ontological premises we introduced. In effect, the theoretical observation of social communication cannot take place anymore within the disciplinary, methodological and epistemological framework of *sociology*. The new assumptions call for the renewal of almost all problem positions within the science of the social which takes from now on the form of a *theory of society*[9] with both terms engulfing each other and

---

9   The topic of the replacement of sociology through a theory of society gains decisive momentum in Luhmann's work from *Soziale Systeme* (1984) onward. Sociolo-

leading to a form of inquiry which could be described with Luhmann as the design of a supertheory.

Both society and theory have undergone structural changes over the past decades. We will have to look at these changes in order to see if they can be put in relation to each other.

Theory

Theory or science is not aware, within its ordinary disciplinary frames, of what is taking place in it. The change in science structure is only partly reflected within science. Chaos, indeterminacy, locality, dissipativity in the realm of experimental and exact science; indeterminacy or "différance" of the signifier in the sciences of meaning, argue in favour of an epistemological revision, but do not bring such a revision forth in full shape. One will have to theoretise the change in the construction of science itself, in the design of its theories to initiate such a revision. Systems theory and the logic of form are powerful theoretical devices that can be fused into a decisive (radical) constructivist scheme reflecting upon the process of science making. The privileged field of such a constructivist approach is a theory of society, which reflects the changes of both terms constituting it.

Science is understood within the framework of such a theory as the first term of a self-engulfing relationship of theoretical observation on the one side and the social communication processes in which it takes place on the other. It is then a specific form of observation giving to apprehension aspects of the world by drawing distinctions on its surface. These distinctions structure the catenation of all concrete, particular acts of scientific observation. Such a radical constructivist approach is then able to explain the growth to the extreme of the capacity of object resolution of scientific theorising as an effect of the contingency and ephemerality of scientific observation itself. It enhances the consciousness of the contingency, paradigm relativity, falsifiability, provisionality of scientific knowledge and its theorematical formulations.

gy is presented in the inaugural chapter of this work as a repetition of the classics (of sociology) and a reappropriation of their theoretical designs.

The enhancement of the object resolution capacity of science[10] does not only mean a improvement in the capacity to approach the object to the limits of its (microscopic) enlargement possibilities – by breaking it into last infinitesimal elements and holes or nothingnesses of discrete non-analysable emptiness correlating to the granularity of the "elemental" object. The constitution of the object is no more external, physical, material; but mental: it is a construction of the object from a variety of scientific, mostly incongruent points of observation. The possibility of variation (contingency) of scientific observation within the range of the discipline concerned and the relevant research programme is that which breaks the firmness of the object and dilutes it, resolves it like a graphic structure with ever-widening resolution capacities.

More precisely, the enhancement of object resolution within scientific observation is an effect of a general widening of the discrepancies between scientific perspectives themselves, a growth of the incongruence of those perspectives. The crossing (cross-breeding) of incongruent perspectives is the most productive device of science today. It is, one could say, the unique form of heuresis that we can use in our knowledge situation today. Incongruence, however, is a very counter-intuitive fact and scientists are mostly not aware of it, taking their cue from older scientific ideals of maximal consistency and closure of any theoretical form of knowledge.

Society

If we understand – with Luhmann – society as communication, that means as a meaning system – or the other meaning system beside consciousness – then society is nothing else than an intersubjective meaning poiesis (Sinnpoiese). Ultimately, society is, when one radicalises the Luhmannian position we are referring to, the one and only

---

10 The idea of an object resolution capacity of science and of its growth I borrow from Luhmann (especially in his *Die Wissenschaft der Gesellschaft*, Frankfurt, Suhrkamp 1990) and try to systematise it. It seems to me to be one of the most interesting motives of a post-ontological epistemology.

meaning poiesis. Consciousness as the other system is not one in which meaning poiesis can be operated autonomously within a closure separating it from communication. Closed conscious meaning poiesis would be radically autistic: averbal, asemantic, substantiated only by perception and "Stimmung" with no semantic articulation. Society would then have to be understood as the only productive emissory processor of meaning – consciousness would be the receptive system, the digesting one, the one in which communication is consummated in the form of lived experience (Erlebnis)[11].

As a meaning poiesis society processes self-distanciating forms of observation, that is of operations whose effectuation mediates the givenness of any object or segment of the world. In contrast, life is a different basic poiesis[12] processing metabolic, convulsive forms of observation[13] based on a specific non-distanciating form of "knowledge" operated within actual syntheseis by which the environment is immediately represented within the biological system, irritating it and urging it to reproduce its elements in cyclical catenations of operations. While life has a scope of operation restricted to the immediate representation of its environments in itself, the boundaries of the

---

11   On the problem of the coupling of communication and consciousness and the autistic structure of the latter, see the creative thesis of Peter Fuchs in his *Die Umschrift: Zwei kommunikationstheoretische Studien: "japanische Kommunikation" und "Autismus"*, Frankfurt, Suhrkamp 1995.

12   I introduced a differentiation between basic and derivative autopoiesis in my: "The Specific Autopoiesis of Law: between Derivative Autonomy and Generalised Paradox". In Priban, Jiri, Nelken, David (eds.): *Law's New Boundaries: The Consequences of Legal Autopoiesis*, Aldershot, Ashgate Publishers 2001, p. 45-79.

13   I have in different contributions explained my understanding of the concept of observation and the necessity to guarantee it maximal inclusiveness in a manner that would make it include operations of biological poiesis and not only cognitive nor specific knowledge operations. I thus go along with Maturana's contention that life also is cognition, reverting however the terms and considering cognition as well as life as operations of distinction discriminating changes in the environment of the system. Observation is thus coextensive with system actuality as such or the mere capacity of a system to posit itself in a continued and enhanced difference to an environment, this being a constitutive property of merely physical systems. A detailed discussion of the question can be found in my: Probleme der Kopplung von Nur-Operationen. Kopplung, Verwerfung, Verdünnung? In *Soziale Systeme*, 7 / 2001-2: 222- 240.

social meaning poiesis are never encountered. There is no outside of the social poiesis of meaning as the unbounded whole of intersubjective meaning production. The world is the only engulfing horizon of such a poiesis, the world being the limit of all distinctions and being itself none. That means that society as the whole of communication is the whole of meaning and the whole of meaningful observation. Such a whole is not a totality. All systemic wholes are localities, more precisely self-engulfing localities. Society encounters the whole of the observable as its correlate, the whole of the observable being a local multiplicity of spaces opened by projected distinctions.

Observation and its observable cannot happen, come to pass, take place, have event, if the difference with which they correlate or out of which they are generated does not make a difference. To make a difference is not to be indifferent for a being capable of interest – to use a Heideggerian phrase: "dem es in ihm selbst um etwas geht". An existential interest, that means a capacity to be concerned – "angegangen" – by the introduction in the world or the drawing on its surface of differences is a structural correlate to observation and the observable. Society is thus a body vibrating with the incidence on its interest-surface, on its world sensibility, of distinctions, differences to which it cannot remain indifferent. This builds the matrix for a structure of self-sensibility, which protracts the meaning poiesis indefinitely.

Production of information (that is of any cognitive or affective surprise, improbability or non-redundancy) is indefinitely self-regenerating since the incidence of a difference resonates on itself: by falling within society a difference (a non-indifference) transforms society and reacts thus to itself. The incidence of information is not only the incidence of the new, which is registered by social communication as such. It is the incidence of the incidence on the subject which is crucial here. Society is thus always resonating with its own differences in a process of self-sensibility, which makes of it a generator of new reactions to the incidence of the new. Every incidence of the new brings society into vibration: novity as the incidence of the new itself generates an apperception and a perception of this incidence itself.

Society's sensible body resonates with novity as society / social communication becomes the spectacle of itself. Novity is a mechanism immanent to social communication, erasing any distinction or limit between the world whole in its actuality and the local whole of social communication. Communication thus becomes its one and only object and theme. It is the "difference" (in the sense of the non-indifference) to its own differences: it differs from each of them, the incidence of each of them on it generating the observation of this incidence itself. Communication lives then from its own spectacle[14].

Contents as such do not count for much. Events – the event of a difference in its incidence and the event of a new difference through this incidence – are the substance of society in the sense of a process of resonating and of a self-sensibility actuated by novity as incidence of information or non-redundancy.

This leads to the very modern phenomenon of societalisation of all that happens in the world – which is then the world of society. Society thus gains a sort of total responsibility for all that occurs – all that is observed by it, or simply all the observed: all that is constructed within communication seems to fall into the domain of that which can be regulated by communication. Society thus accomplishes a sort of total ascription to itself of all causality – even something like nature (as a antithesis to society), and here especially wild nature, is ultimately a construct of communication as its is operating its meaning poieseis. Equipped with a very dense network of continuously operating mass media, society appears to itself as the resonating, self-sensible, all encompassing, self-engulfing imago of local totality.

A theory of society

Under these circumstances, a theory of society is the product of an operating subsystem of society itself, the scientific subsystem, and within this subsystem of a particular discipline or complex of disci-

---

14 On self-sensibility of certain media, see my theoretical developments throughout *Sciences du sens. Perspectives théoriques.* Strasbourg Presses Universitaires de Strasbourg 2006.

plines: the social sciences. Such a scientific observation of society is constituted by a bundle of networked communication strings, organised in adequacy to the standards of the type of scientific communication within the social sciences. Within this segment of communication, the whole of communication is observed as such. Such a whole being the whole of observation as all encompassing meaning poiesis as such, its reflection within a segment of it that cannot by principle nor by a precise criterion be distinguished from it entails a structure of paradoxical entangling.

There exists no meta-language that is able to disentangle the segment from the whole and conversely[15]. If contents / objects can bear an index of order indicating a structural level of reflexivity, events cannot. There is no possibility and no criterion to distinguish incidences of differences and to differentiate novities as such. There is no difference of plane between social meaning poiesis and scientific meaning poiesis[16].

To put science and society in relation to any other term brings this term into a "Gödelisation" or paradoxical entanglement with the former. The more so, when science and society are related to each other. Society and science are terms engulfing themselves and everything that enters in a ratio with them. This is what recent science studies have shown. In the perspective of science studies – as well as of a systems theoretical sociology of science -, there can be no point of observation of science from which science could be observed before its entanglement with society or from which such an entanglement could be neutralised or its effects reversed or discounted. The engulfment of science by society reveals science to be a contingent effect of processes of social communication, which cannot cease to operate in any

---

15 A theory of types is quite inadequate for such a purpose, because it can only mark contents and not events.

16 Lacan's thesis of the non-existence of a meta-language (capable of overseeing the language of the unconscious in us) can be linked to mine in a very pregnant way. I prefer not to develop here the transition to Lacan because the position of the latter should be worked out in order to show the consistency of the link. This would lead us away from our present concerns.

operation of observation, especially not that operation by which the relationship of science to those processes themselves is observed. In this respect, there is no site beyond these processes where a theory of the entanglement of science and society could establish itself. The observation of the entanglement itself is entangled in it.

In a theoretical and cultural setting determined by an irresistible recognition of the overwhelming power of paradoxising "Gödelising" figures engulfing all orders of meaning there is no possibility to distinguish, in the iterated reversals of sameness and otherness, an inside and an outside of these orders. This is a major avenue of de-ontologisation, transforming as well the world of cognition as the substance and architecture of social normativities.

Denomination

I would like now to reflect upon the logical structure of self-engulfing terms and their Gödelising effects on one another when they are set into relation to one another. We have encountered these figures of post-ontological paradoxising at their most stringent site, that is in the entanglement of theoretical observation with social communication, of science and society. Our conclusion was that there is no metalanguage, only events, production of surprise and novity. This entails a new structure of knowledge based on the crossing of contingent, plural and incongruent distinctions. It is this structure that I now would like to comment upon.

In traditional logic, terms are conceived of as identities and unities that can be simply put or posited as such. God, man, bed, white, mortal... are such terms. They can take their place in enunciation as subjects (substantives) or as predicates (attributes).

Their entity is not touched, not influenced by co-position of other terms. When multiple terms occur in a position of thinking - while they are thought of, in a act of noein – they do not interfere as to change something into something else.

When multiple terms occur in a position in which they are thought of as belonging to the same multiplicity, then a space is imagined which is that of a set that has a number of elements. An abstract operation allows the building of a set that has no other element than one term. Still more abstract is the construction of a set that has no element at all.

This extremely short reminder of Aristotelian and set theoretical basics are intended as an introduction to the making of one operation, that of putting a term at the denominator of another one.

We are proceeding with so many precautions because there are different ways to operate a de-nomination. Most generally it is to put one designed term into relation to another designed term. Such a relation can be totally external, i.e. leaving unaltered the terms entering into relation, like that of building sets mentioned above. It is then the very elementary relationship of belonging to a set.

Other relations can be more complex. Multiplication brings together a term designed to be multiplied with another term designed to be its multiplicator. The terms remain unaltered: they however give rise to a third term, which is their product. There are lots of mathematical operations applied to mathematical entities like numbers, which give birth to third terms as a result of their bringing to operation two or more terms at the places left and right of their operators.

Most complex are operations of relationing (putting into relation), which alter the terms in a way that these loose their self-identity. They cannot anymore be supposed to "endure" as that what they are. The relation is no more external to its objects: it is immanent to them and constitutive of their dynamic identity. Such are the operations of dialectical logics where no term can be anymore supposed to exist as self-identical. Every term is immanently relational and refers to a dialectical counterpart with which it is dynamically intertwined. Terms have or are then histories into which they are bound to unfold.

Mathematical and philosophical interests brought up an evolution that de-substantified terms or positions through a broadening of the set of objectivities that could be termed or posited. So terms (substantives) could not anymore be set in opposition to relations (verbs), because relations, functions, operations etc. were put themselves as terms or arguments of higher order relations, functions, etc.

Most revolutionary were recent attempts to de-ontologise logic in a way as to make it shift from a logic of identity to a logic of difference. George Spencer Brown's *Laws of form* is paradigmatic of such attempts. By triggering discussions and debates in the sphere of arts and social sciences, it could influence modes of thinking concerning how such a shift could be accomplished within these sciences.

The mark Spencer Brown made use of to posit an element (form) did not pass between two pre-existing terms but through a single element, thus giving birth to it against the background of all that it is not. A form (a term) is thus two-sided with a designated, "indicated" and a non-indicated side. Self is a separation mark between self and non-self. Since self is the separation as well as the separated, than self is always re-introduced in itself as the difference that it is. It is infinitely self-recurrent in itself.

Jacques Lacan developed a very idiosyncrasic mathematics of desire built around short formulas which he called *mathèmes* ("mathemes"). Central to such a mathematics is a mark called "barre" under which denominators could be put in relation to nominator terms. The meaning of the Lacanian "barre" is variable in relation to the terms that it separates. Sometimes it crosses, "bars" a single term and means its splitting.

Now I would like to introduce a particular use of the dividing mark (bringing two terms into a relation of division). This use is not dialectic. It builds on the logics of Spencer Brown and the mathemes of Jacques Lacan, in the sense that it is strictly de-ontologising. What is put at the bottom of the fraction[17] is the term that would engulf itself and the nominator in an entanglement that ruins all discontinuity and identity between the terms.

---

17 "Our word *fraction* did not originally have a mathematical sense. It goes back ultimately to the Latin verb *frangere*, "to break." From the stem of the past participle *frāctus* is derived Late Latin *frāctiō* (stem *frāctiōn-*), "a breaking" or "a breaking in pieces," as in the breaking of the Eucharistic Host. In Medieval Latin the word *frāctiō* developed its mathematical sense, which was taken into Middle English along with the word. The earliest recorded sense of our word is "an aliquot part of a unit, a fraction or subdivision," found in a work by Chaucer written about 1400. One of the next recorded instances of the word recalls its origins, referring to the "brekying or fraccioun" of a bone" (Webster's Dictionary).

The argument of the entanglement of science and society developed above hints at such a denomination with the particularity that each term can be set at the bottom of the other. It is the setting of a term at the bottom that is decisive because it is in such a position that incalculable or "irrational" denominators reveal themselves as such. This makes it impossible to reach a "rational" product of the operation of division at stakes. They show that the sort of proportionality postulated between the terms has no determinate value, but iterates the fraction of each term through the other through their mutual entanglement.

However denomination has not only to do with "incalculable" terms. Even when terms are circumscribable, denomination reveals the gliding of the fraction mark through them, the relativity and contingency not only of their proportionality, but also of each term taken for itself. It deconstructs the identity, closure and firmness of any term, showing it as a simple effect of meaning, and not as a pre-given, already constituted, unitary content. It shows that any term is the product of a preceding denomination, which is not visible anymore in it. In this sense, it reproduces the movement of difference accomplished typically as the emergence and articulation of meaning itself. It enacts the gliding of the signifier and gives it as the sole horizon of cognition and thought. As enactment of matters that have come to a stasis and that occult therewith the movement to their own emergence, it brings to manifestation the general incalculability of any term put at the bottom of its bar. The advent of any term to its stasis and self-identity obscures the entanglements of the fraction, of the operation and event of splitting and gliding which it is.

Denomination has to be revealed as the basic operation of any meaning projection, its main potentiality being to denominate denominators in gliding operation whose actual effectuation is a sort of absolute present that cannot be relativised. One cannot go beyond the denomination, which is effectuated at present, *actu*, and project other, possible alternatives to it, nor anticipate possible subsequent denominations of it. This explains the very firmness of the operation of denomination itself, which cannot be reduced to a general syntax or algorithm producing an open multiplicity of possible intellections. The present of denomination-intellection is axial and axially saturated. It can neither be generalised nor formalised.

Denomination is then a productive intellective operation which lives from the tension produced by the introduction of a difference between nominator and denominator and the reintroduction of this difference within the denominator as the term engulfing the other, that means the term able to reflect its difference to the nominator in itself. It is a major figure of thought in our present epistemic constitution giving rise to a form of post-ontological intellection parting from intuition and comprehension, soliciting improbable constructions with very high potentials of cognitive surprise. The exposure of a term to the effects of its fraction by another is a sort of metaphorising, which inflects its original paths of signification and reshape the whole chart of its expansion.

The heuristic dynamics of denomination

Science is a type of cognitive surprise, which is organised around a body of operations of distinctions or more precisely around a modus of bringing forth such differences with non-redundant, informative "content". This process is not metalinguistically distinguishable from what is going on in meaning poiesis at large.

If we look at how science is produced today – restricting our scope to arts and social sciences – we can observe, considering for instance the titles of books published by university presses, that it is generated by a matrix of combination or relationing of more or less openly incongruent objects or incongruent perspectives upon objects[18]. This relationing I formalise as an operation of denomination putting a

---

18   English titles of social science and arts books tend to be, since a couple of decades, very elegant, poetic ones. They almost always make use of surprising associations, inventive word inversions, elaborate preciosity in contrasting title and sub-title – the result being mostly a disappointment by what is behind the titles, in the prosaic bulk of the book. The impression is sometimes that the whole cue of the book

term, which would be the inventive, heuristically more potent term below another one, which is the principal object, assumed as known by common or special (scientific) knowledge. The nominator functions like the more static term of the relation. I propose to call it the plain term of it. Some denominations relate or divide or fraction terms whose discrepancy in plainness is very small: if the denominator is almost as plain or as static as the nominator, then the denomination is redundant, poorly informative, purely reproductive in style. It reproduces with no significant variation conventional object constructions and remains within a bulk of conform perspectives. It is only when variance as a quality of non-conform perspectives is introduced that heuristic potentiality emerges.

Finally, it should be very heavily stressed that novity and heuristic superiority of denominations by no means imply that those denominations themselves are really and contentfully superior to others, i.e. that they are substantially more valuable and deliver a denser "knowledge" than others. What is here indicated, differentiated or roughly measured are cognitive surprise qualities of events and not qualifications of their correlated contents. To distinguish here between event and content, privileging the content side as the substantial, semantic or theorematic result of the process, would bring us back to a theoretical level which has been especially and very consistently transcended by our conception of denomination. This conception presupposes a post-ontological setting in which there are only operations, events, the coming to pass of differences. Their substantial, final products, their stabilised, objectified and closed outcomes in semantic unities (of things, concepts, functions) have no special relevance. No site of observation can be given, no metalanguage is available which would deliver a measure of comparison of insights produced by denominations. Their validity in terms of absolute cognitive gains or increments cannot be assessed. Only their denominational

is the title itself as the acme of the heuristic impulse of the inquiry. The crossing of incongruent perspectives is namely most elegantly performed by the title, while the book cannot hold the promise of such a heuristic tension. It falls down from it and reverts to more conform ways of contextualisation and denomination.

intensity can be compared. The further measure of their intellective intensity is that of their capacities of connection, catenation, condensation and confirmation within constituted bodies of experience and cognition. Ultimately they would reach a level of consistency, which is that of a theory organising those denominations in a circular and productive scheme.

To give an idea of the different intensities of denomination, I propose the construction of an example illustrating the different levels of heuristic potential. I put in the nominator position, that of the plain term, the nominal historic entity 'Peloponnesian war'. A case of reproductive denomination would put below this plain term that of 'political transformations' bringing the first term in historical, causal, motivational, circumstantial etc. relation with the second (the introduced denominator). This would announce a study of the consequences of the war on the political regimes, institutions, settings, power relations within and between the Greek cities taking part in it. In the denomination both objects are more or less static, their crossing does not bear any significant divergence from the bulk of constituted knowledge. In contrast, denominating or breaking (fracting, diffracting) the Peloponnesian war through a term like gender, (ecological) environment or ethnicity would enhance the informative potential through its own improbability or novity. Traditional historiography (Thucydides), classical history (until Rollin), scientific historical inquiry (of the 19th and part of the 20th century) could not push their thematics to a point where gender, ecology and ethnicity as such could be set in a relevant, significant relationship to such an object as the Peloponnesian war[19]. The improbability or the novity of the relationing would reach very high levels with the introduction under the same plain term of denominators like information distribution, decision praxis, computational skills of actors etc. Beyond this peak of heuristic tension a bifurcation would then occur, leading on the one side to crossings

---

19   Scientific (historical) inquiry of the 19th and 20th century occasionally pointed out the "modernity" of Thucydides as a historian or that of the Greek man emerging from the long strife between the cities.

which would be felt as so bizarre that they would succumb to irrelevance; and on the other to a particularly tense irritation of the receptivity to the inventive potential of meaning projections in the vicinity of the theme defined by the nominator.

Another example would be the denomination of museum through money. We all go to museums, know museums as mostly public institutions, supported by public funds. Museums exhibit art works, which are thought of as disinterested works, occupying a privileged and highly valued space which is severed from the profit logics of the economy. At some moment, a business school student has the idea to write a dissertation on the profitability/cost-effectiveness of museums. Doing so, she denominates 'museum' with money and tries to think a museum in terms of transaction costs and reconstruct the evolution towards the musealisation of art works in that perspective. Proceeding this way, she dares to open an unfamiliar perspective crossing the self-evidence and obviousness of the existence of museums and their being decoupled from economy, with an incongruent relationship to money... Similar approaches of law and even sex[20] in terms of rational and economic choice belong to the same vein. The rational choice approach of law in particular inaugurated the genre of such denominations of self-evidently autonomous social fields by the rationality of choice understood as always oriented towards cost-benefit assessments. The repetition of such a denomination densifies its lines of fraction and brings about a sort of matrix of observation of fields of social action through the prisms of economic transaction costs. Ultimately, the repetition will erode the heuristic intensity of the denomination and provoke a fatigue, a wearing out of its intellective momentum. The denomination loses its inaugural effect, i.e. that of being effectuated for the first time, or of being applied first-hand to a new material field. It is then perceived as just one new application of a scheme, which has, through its repeated applications themselves, already lost its novity or more precisely its novity effectiveness as an

---

20   Like in Richard Posner's *Sex and Reason*. Cambridge Mass., Harvard University Press 1992.

opening of intellective potential[21]. Novity is thus a structural moment of the event of intellection itself.

More examples of denomination are now provided in order to show the direction taken by cognitive projections under the pressure of this novity moment – i.e. the pressure born from the necessity of its production, in high intensities, in any intellective endeavour. Denominating water through war (water/war) would at first sight bring into relation water observed as a scarce resource in connection with war, because such a vital and scarce resource has been fought for at numerous junctures in history. Now, denomination gain in heuristic intensity by being introduced in very light contexts, I mean contexts which are very poorly determining. The tendency of contemporary intellection is thus to minimise context circumstantiation and determination, ultimately setting the denomination *per se* with very few additional instantiations.

Deconstructing or neutralising contexts is a device of re-opening potentials of novity for a denomination of terms, which would otherwise glide into conventional ways of thematic association. It lets a denomination stand for itself on a vast floor of potential, but non-determined, non-fostered, non-probabilised intellections. Conform spontaneous context building which would shift continuation and further connections of the denomination into preferential directions, probabilised by the sole inertia of already 'loaded', 'condensed' intellection patterns. The alighting of context and the per se position of a denomination denudes it from pre-structuring and prevailing substantiations. When nudity is reached, even the plain term loses its stasis. The denomination enters, in its both terms, into a space of estrangement. It loses any self-evidence and tends to become reversible.

Out of such a context suspension (epochè) emerges at first a sort of

---

21 If you look at the gender discussion today, the tension of the denomination politics / women has reached some high degree of fatigue within certain audiences. The literary "primeur" of the denomination could be enjoyed by a work like *The Bostonians*. Contemporary works with a comparable thematic have to exploit other, secondary, e.g. psychoanalytic perspectives, thus untying its strict bonds to the standard political debate.

nearly compulsive reversion of the denomination. It is the first event that tends to take place on the new, denuded floor of intellection. What is 'done' is an inversion of the fraction, with the plain term coming in the position of the denominator. Both terms gain a sort of equal strangeness from the suspension of contextual conformity. They are equally "unstatic", improbable, versatile, invention oriented, and they show it by exchanging their places. When a denomination is "suspended" (so to say: in the air), it generates internal tension, with the propensity to groundless reversals of its terms. Its fraction itself becomes unstable, mobile, turning upside down. Both terms enter in a movement of recession leading them back to the extreme nudity of a signifier. They are stripped from their plain denotations and regress to the status of uncertain, merely relational or differential entities, existing or emerging to effectiveness through the condensation of some of their associational potentials. These happen to overlap in a way as to give shape to an actual relationing, exerting its tension and cohesive power as long as the operations in which it is effectuated sustain themselves as part of a living intellective process, event, happening. This dynamics delivers the reversed denomination war/water and the perspective of a relationing bringing to stand a transience of war through water. Jacques Derrida would have seen no objection to speak, quite extensively, about a sort of watering war. Water and war are separated or denominated, as signifiers, graphically by the difference and interplay of two letters, phonetically by a quasi-syllable. They are thus held in a proximity, which furthers all sorts of reversals of their relationing. The originary denomination water/war has been dynamised by the suspension of both terms and their relationship in a nudeness they acquire when they recess to an ultimate signifier status. The new dynamic is purely associational and pertain to a sort of intellective poetics[22].

22 One would have to experiment or "play" with whole series of examples in order to precise the outlook on such a theory of denomination / intellection. It is always important to begin with intuitive denominations and to let them progressively drift away or back to the planes of their signifier-terms. A denomination capital

Corpus and transience

I would like to introduce at this juncture some terminological conventions designed to facilitate the further inspection of the dynamics of denomination-intellection. I call *corpus* the plain term or the nominator of a cognitive relationing. I call *transient* the denominator which (dif)fracts the corpus[23]. The use of such a metaphorics of corporeity and transience, of corporeal cohesion and fracting legitimates itself because of a structural movement occurring within every denomination and leading to the corporisation of fractions or denominations themselves taken as wholes and their renewed fraction through new transients.

The process by which a denomination wears out and fatigues its inventivity leads to a tendency which fosters the emergence of a new corpus constituted by the old corpus and the old transient of the original denomination. This reflects the process of familiarisation and habitualisation of every perspective of observation: it ages, matures, is eroded, loses its information and surprise momentum. With increasing erosion of this momentum, the relation between the nominator and denominator cannot be distinguished any more from that of

(city) / war for instance would at first exert an intuitive inventivity, showing how wars "fabricate" capitals (from ancient times onward, capitals being ceremonial centres where gods can be worshipped, where people can bring their offerings and let them be handled like capital deposits, where states emerge with centres of decision and command). The reversed denomination would show how capitals fabricate wars, being the centres of radiation of power as cohesive power. Transitional toward signifier associations would be the understanding of capital as an economic regime having at its core a capitalist one (although there may exist non-capitalist capitals); also transitional the exploration of war as capital, something which can be placed, invested, can fructify and deliver added power value along the principles of a polemic economy. On the plane of the signifier, one of numerous, indefinite associations would be that of war and waste (gastina) as the reversal of the figure itself of a capital.

23 I have been working out these concepts for some time and was stunned when I came across a text of Teilhard de Chardin where not only the – truly unusual – concept of transience but also that – not less unusual – of corpus (corps) are successively introduced. I would have liked to bring homage to Teilhard – a writer I most deeply admire – for the prime authorship of this conceptuality. However the meaning I endow both concepts with is actually quite remote from that adopted for them by Teilhard. Teilhard's text is *Le phénomène humain*, Paris Seuil 1959, p. 49 sq.

signifier and signified within the unity of the sign, as Saussure under-
stands it. Such a sign is, in Saussure's theory, a double-faced entity,
whose faces (signifier and signified) are not split in a manner that
would enable them to exist apart from each other. The sign, like a
sheet of paper, is the double-faced unity of a dichotomous entity. At
its origin however a sign is a venture, an invention, a special, progressively pronouncing articulation, an inaugurally daring association of a signifier with a signified – of a sound with a meaning, in ver-
bal language. This original and inventive moment of the sign structure is that which first recedes into latency. What remains is a wholly
habitualised combination of both terms, yielding a firm unity that
cannot be imagined to having been split. Repetition, habitualisation
and redundancy however elicit a decline in signification or semiolog-
ical vividness, which has an effect on the sign. So, even if the spontaneous tendency of the sign is to rigidify and occult the combination of
signifier and signified out of which it is born, such a tendency cannot
be indefinitely effective. The movement is thus double: unification
and rigidification – we shall call it corporisation in the following – on
the one side; re-splitting and re-combination on the other. The second
movement is that of the metaphorisation of all significance by which
a sign is able to signify. Signs can never be univocal, because they
have always already mobilised a stream of associative significance
transient under their seemingly substantial and semantically bounded unities. The transience of a crossed metaphorical signification is
that which metaphorises signification and maintains the whole of it in
mobility and inventivity.

The new transient would then split the corporised whole of the old
denomination along lines – you can call them distinctions, differences, signi-fications – of its own. The new splitting constitutes the
emergence of a new denomination, with the actual vividness of its
effectuation as a relationing of nominator and denominator in a association with heuristic tension. Such a process is constantly on-going
and represents the regeneration of the medium of meaning threatened by erosion and fatigue through conformity and redundancy of

the distinction praxis of the discourse at stake. However, the advent of such a denomination must be probabilised by something, which accounts for the necessity to distinguish along this distinction. As we have seen, there is no possible grounding of such distinctions in necessity. A denomination is, at high levels of heuristic intensity, mostly inaugural of its own fertility, vividness of insight, plausibility of confirmed contents. A denomination is not a proposition, nor a judgment, nor theorem. It is an intellective event producing a potential of vivid cognitive experience.

Intellection and theory

We could now try to situate the concept of theory as a formalised intellection within the framework we have been working out. Theory has to be understood as a modus of denomination which itself has to be constituted as a macro-corpus requiring very high consistency and delivering an attractor for all heuresis, for all processes of invention taking place in its vicinity. A theory stands on the ground of a number of denominations with very high cohesive force as well as very high heuristic tension. In these denominations nominators are attached very strictly to their denominators and determine a series of further denominations connected to them in a self-inclusive, cyclical and circular manner, delivering the axiomatical or doctrinal or evidential foundations of the theory. The principal denominations upon which the theory rests as well as their firm connection with one another undergo a process of (macro-) corporisation by which they tend to build a perfected whole. The lines of fracture of the fundamental denominations are not visible anymore. These build constituted unities of significance and do not let themselves be split anymore along their mark of division. The connection of those denominations to a whole of principles (*principia, initia,* Anfangsgründe, maxims, postulates, doctrinal sentences, Lehrsätze, *lemmata…*) is a sort of multiple denomination of denominations. Within the macro-denomination corporisa-

205

tion is at work and leads, through a process of erasure of denominational fraction lines, to the consolidation, crystallisation, unification,
closure of a macro-corpus building the core of a theory which unfolds
with the transience of all possible objects through the corpus.

Like any entity, theory can be observed, within a theory-theoreti-
cal framework, as a constituted body of distinctions, which are maintained in operation by the transience through them of more or less
conform terms or objects. Thus, theory is nothing else than an organising body of corpus-transience operations of relationing. Every theory crystallises for itself a specific mode of transience - or a small numbers of transience modi – which is maintained in operation as long as
the theory is able to produce intellection. That means as long as cognitive acts with high intensities of innovative surprise can be enacted
within the domain of its operation. Thus a theory tends, with its corporised body of leading or basic distinctions and their circular connections, to constitute a thinking machine, producing intellection on
a current basis. A theory is a matrix of intellective operations exerting
an attraction on any relationing of terms taking place within a perime-
ter to which its potency to function as a model or assimilator for
diverse types of meaning projections stretches.

When theory reaches a very high consistency and organises itself
systematically with its own architectonics and its own relations of
doctrinal programme und implementation[24], it acquires a puzzling
autonomy and the self-standing status of a mundane entity. It can
gain a sort of unchallengeability for instance (in the case of the thinking paradigms of Hegel, Darwin and Freud) or high attractiveness[25]
building a constraint to think within its categories and along its distinctions, applying its forms to the intellective space which it opens
and explores. It structures and organises it in a manner that restricts
its access to modi of transience of its own.

---

24 It is what german idealism conceptualised at the beginning of the 19th century as
    the dichotomy of *Darstellung* und *Ausführung*.

25 Luhmann's theory is a case of high – almost irresistible – attractiveness. It is not a
    constraining thinking machine, but a matrix of knowledge production by all
    means.

Gunther Teubner, speaking on one occasion of Latourian hybrids[26], went so far as to cite theories among the objects belonging to such a set of beings. A theory is a hybrid in the sense that it is a body of deixeis taking form in scriptural formulations reflecting originary intellections offered to be appropriated by a multiplicity of intellects organising their intellective operations in a manner specific for the theory. The existence of a theory enables a community of such intellects to indicate the world along the same lines of denomination. Theory offers a redundant way to denominate "things" through transient others[27]. A theory is then the organisation of transience modi, which structures the place of a "thing" at the confluence of all its uses as the paths to it.

While reaching extremely high levels of coherence, explanation power and closure, a theory is able to constitute a sort of totally self-sustaining, self-centred otherness and to swallow, like the eye of a whirlpool, the whole (local) universe surrounding it. Its potency can be uncanny, giving it a sort of existence outside of the intelligent operator operating it, centred in its own corpus (of fundamental distinctions und their circular organisation) as the almost monadological focus of its whole world projection. Theory can thus be seen as a centre of reflection, specular convergence and vision outside of the intelligent operator, having subsistence independently from him. It is like an eye, which subsists beyond him, actually looks at him with the full firmness and sharpness of intellective actual autarchy. The landscape appears as still more threatening when one considers not only one single theory, but a multiplicity of such, each presenting the observer with a similar central focalisation or occularisation so to say of intellection. The vision of a heterotopia emerges then, which fragments

---

26 At the Conference 'Normativities: Law, Science and "Society"', org. A. Bora, A. Pottage, Zentrum für Interdisziplinäre Forschung (Zif) Bielefeld, 7-9 July 2005. His contribution is forthcoming in a special issue of the *Zeitschrift für Rechtssoziologie* 2006.
27 There are no "things" as such. It is the operative, redundant use of things, of their names, definitions, differences to other things within operations of denomination that constitutes "things" for a theoretical observation.

the world in a series of local universes, which cannot be unified nor organised in a functional, organic, hierarchical nor formal manner.

Notes on Contributors

Dirk Baecker, Dr. rer.soc., Professor for Cultural Theory and Analysis at zeppelin university, Friedrichshafen/Bodensee. Areas of work: sociological theory, sociology of society and culture, economic sociology, organization research, management teaching. See most recently *Form und Formen der Kommunikation* (Suhrkamp 2005) and *Wozu Gesellschaft?* (Berlin 2007).

Jean Clam, Research Fellow at Centre National de la Recherche Scientifique (Paris/France). His current affiliation is the Centre Marc Bloch in Berlin. He is trained as philosopher, sociologist and psychologist. His recent books include: *Trajectoires de l'immatériel. Contributions à une théorie de la valeur et de sa dématérialisation* (Paris 2004); *Kontingenz, Paradox, Nur-Vollzug. Grundprobleme einer Theorie der Gesellschaft* (Konstanz 2004) and *Sciences du sens. Perspectives théoriques* (Strasbourg 2006).

Niels Lehmann, Associate Professor at and currently head of the Institute of Aesthetic Studies, University of Aarhus. He is trained as a dramaturg. His main field of study is performance aesthetics and the various theories of difference, which inform this branch of the art world.

Lars Qvortrup, 1996-2000 professor at the Department of Communication, Aalborg University, 2000-2007 professor at the Department of Literature, Culture and Media, University of Southern Denmark, since 2007 rector at the Royal School of Library and Information Science. His recent books include *The Hypercomplex Society* (2003), *Det* *vidende samfund* [The Knowing Society] (2004) and *Knowledge, Education and Learning – E-learning in the Knowledge Society* (2006).

Bo Kampmann Walther, Associate Professor at the Department of Literature, Culture and Media, University of Southern Denmark. He has published extensively on new media, computer games, sports and media, and digital aesthetics. His recent books include *Konvergens og nye medier* [Convergence and New Media] (2005) and *Madridismo: En bog om Real Madrid* [Madridismo: A book about Real Madrid] (2006).